The Kingdom of God is like a Yogurt Plant

Selected writings by Bob Jeffery

www.jeffery-archive.net

Jeffery Archive
30a Main Road
Castlehead
Paisley, Scotland.
PA2 6AW

www.jeffery-archive.net

ISBN: 978-1-9997514-0-1
ISBN (eBook): 978-1-9997514-1-8

Typeset by Graham Jeffery, Hilary Jeffery, Nehal McGregor & Inigo Sands
Cover design by Inigo Finn Jeffery Sands
Cover image: *Dean of Worcester*, Charles Jeffery (1993)
Printed by Parchments Print of Oxford Ltd.
1a, Crescent Road, Cowley, Oxford, OX4 9PB

CONTENTS

Foreword

We hope you enjoy reading this small collection of sermons, lectures and writings by Bob Jeffery. They have been selected during the process of sorting through Bob's huge archive. He worked ceaselessly throughout his life towards realising an outward-facing and generous form of Christianity, inspired by the theology of Dietrich Bonhoeffer. Rather than attempting to offer a 'representative selection', we have chosen pieces that caught our attention, addressed recurrent themes in Bob's work, and that seem to retain their resonance and relevance for today.

Bob was born in Hillingdon, on the edge of London in 1935. His parents, Gwenyth and Norman Jeffery, were enthusiastic members of the Scouting movement, and Norman was a senior Tax Inspector. During the Second World War the family moved to Borth-y-Gest in North Wales, as the Inland Revenue relocated its operations to the Imperial Hotel in Llandudno. Following Norman's retirement in 1963, his parents moved back to Borth-y-Gest, where they remained for the rest of their lives. His older sister, Clare (1928 – 1995), had a long career as a theatre designer and educator, working for the Old Vic, the Royal Shakespeare Company, the Royal Court Theatre, Woodfall Films, Manchester Royal Exchange Theatre, at Wimbledon School of Art and the Central School of Speech and Drama.

In the closing years of the War, the family moved back to north west London and Bob subsequently attended preparatory school in Chichester, then St Paul's School, and took a degree in theology at King's College London. In this period, he was also an enthusiastic audience member of London's many Music Halls and became an adept conjuror, studying stage illusions and magic. He later said that this immersion in showmanship stood him in good stead for liturgy: "it's all performance", he would say. He was ordained in 1960, after a period working as an RAF telephonist in Germany as part of his National Service. He served two curacies: at St. Aidan's, Grangetown, Sunderland, and St. Mary, Barnes. For the second half of the 1960s he worked in the heart of the Church's bureaucracy, first as Assistant Secretary of the Mission and Ecumenical Council of the Church Assembly, and later as secretary of the Department of Mission and Unity at the British Council of Churches. (He reflects on this period in the sermon, included in this collection, which marks the 50th anniversary of his ordination.)

Whilst working at Church House in Westminster, he met Ruth Tinling, who was part of the secretarial team for the Board for Mission and

Unity. A great openness of spirit and a shared love of music, literature, theatre, the arts, hospitality - and what Ruth would call 'fresh air' - the great British outdoors - sustained their relationship. They married in 1968 and had four children in relatively quick succession – Graham (b. 1969), Hilary (b. 1971), Philippa (b. 1973) and Charles (b. 1975). In 1971 Bob was appointed Vicar of St. Andrew's, Headington and Rural Dean of Cowley in Oxford, where he stayed until 1978, when he was made Lichfield Diocesan Missioner under Bishop Kenneth Skelton, followed by his appointment as Archdeacon of Salop in 1980. During this period the family lived in the village of Tong, Shropshire. As well as driving hundreds of miles a week as part of his duties as Archdeacon, Bob found time to immerse himself in the intriguing history of the parish for which he was 'Priest in Charge', and began the research which was eventually published as Discovering Tong in his retirement. Through the 1980s, Bob also became increasingly involved in the workings of the Church of England's General Synod, and was elected to the Synod's Standing Committee. In 1987, he was appointed Dean of Worcester, where he led the appeal to save the cathedral tower from collapse and restore the fabric of the building.

The sudden death of Ruth in 1995 (followed by the equally unexpected death of his sister Clare a few weeks later) led to a major change in priorities, and he relinquished many of his outside commitments. In 1996, Bob moved to Christ Church, Oxford, where he remained as Sub-Dean until his retirement in 2002. In 1999, he was awarded an Honorary Doctorate of Divinity by the University of Birmingham. After retirement, he stayed in Oxford, kept busy by scores of projects, speaking and social engagements, and was a frequent contributor to the Church Times and the Expository Times as well as writing numerous clerical obituaries for The Times. Every year he would entertain streams of visitors to his flat in Cowley with food, stories, memories and opinions. He died just after sunrise on 21st December 2016 at Sobell House Hospice, in his old parish of Headington. Right to the last he retained the stoicism, stubbornness, humour, concern for others, historical awareness and literary wit that was such a hallmark of his life's work. According to his wishes, his body is buried in the churchyard at St Bartholomew's, Tong, in an unmarked grave.

Alongside his many professional achievements, Bob also found time to bring up a family with Ruth, and was always there for so many friends and colleagues. We four grew up as a somewhat noisy and unruly crowd in the midst of all this activity, and have put together this book as a small gesture of recognition and gratitude. His legacy is a big one and his writings raise many questions that still need serious thought and attention. For those who wish to look more deeply into Bob's life and work, his archive will be housed at Gladstone's Library in Hawarden, Cheshire, and a list of his main publications is included at the end of this volume. Despite their slightly jarring effect on the reader, we have retained the 'gendered' language in the earlier pieces as it reflects the writing style of the time. Wherever possible, we have tried to include complete references for the works cited in the text. Particular thanks go to Justin Lewis- Anthony for helping us track down sources for some of the more obscure quotations.

We would like to thank our entire family as well as Bob and Ruth's many friends and colleagues who have assisted us in the difficult process of saying goodbye.

Graham, Hilary, Philippa and Charles Jeffery
June 2017

The Kingdom of God is like a Yoghurt Plant

Sermon given at St Paul's School, Connecticut

27 September 2002

The parables of Jesus are based on experiences of everyday life from which quite a lot of other meanings can be drawn. The Biblical commentators are pretty sure that when the Gospels do give an explanation, they are not part of the original text. So I want to tell you a new parable from my own experience and leave you to draw your own conclusions.

Some years ago, at the end of a meeting in my house a friend said to me "Would you like a yoghurt plant?" Not quite knowing what it was, but keen to try it, I was given a demonstration of what to do.

It is a culture, which feeds on milk. The culture I was given was supposed to have come from Imperial Russia in the 1890s - so it had a long history. It needs careful attention. It must never have contact with metal. You put the culture, which looks a bit like dry rice pudding into a glass jar and fill it up with milk. You cover the jar with muslin and leave it in a warm room. After two or three days you take the culture and rub it through a plastic sieve with a wooden spoon. What goes through the sieve is highly edible yoghurt. What remains behind is the culture. You give the culture a wash with cold water and put it back in the jar and start again.

Now comes the interesting part. The culture grows all the time and gets bigger and bigger. So the size or number of jars you use has to increase. The amount of milk you have to use gets more and more. In a state of panic, you have visions of the yoghurt plant taking over your whole home and almost being swallowed up by it.

There is only one solution. You have to keep on giving it away. So around the parish I was in, more and more people had yoghurt plants, which they were also trying to give away to each other. My curate took a service once a week in a convent and he took some down there. So that it is now part of the staple diet of the nuns. A couple of years later I met someone in Scotland who had been given some yoghurt culture by the nuns.

The plant still had to be cared for. It dies if you leave it too long. If you go away on holiday you can leave the culture in the fridge and start it up again when you return. You have to be very careful not to let it get in any contact with metal or it just dies. The only thing to do is to keep on giving it away. But that is not the end of the story.

About two years later I came across a letter in a London newspaper, which read as follows:

Dear Sir, in an idle moment I glanced through the Financial Section of your paper. My attention was caught by the drawing of a tub called 'Natural Yoghurt' in Francis Kinsman's article. Curiosity aroused, I started to read. Yoghurt is a common soured milk product on sale in the United Kingdom but the soured milk made by Francis Kinsman is not yoghurt. Correctly it should be called 'kefir' and so made by a kefir plant or kefir grains. For this is the name of the white tapioca-like granules. On several occasions over the past few years I have become aware of that home brewed was being made by various people and incorrectly called yoghurt. To the layman the difference between the two products appears to be trivial. Yoghurt is milk soured by a lactobacillus and streptococcus growing together for six to eight hours at a temperature of 25 degrees centigrade. The latter product is less acid than yoghurt, should be slightly gassy and taste detectable ethanol (alcohol). Perhaps the difference between kefir and yoghurt is unnoticed because the acidity of the latter is often masked by added sugar or fruit.

So it is not what I thought it was anyhow. But that is not the end of the story. A couple of years later, not having been swamped by the kefir plant we went away on holiday and left the culture in a jar in the freezer. Someone was staying in the house to look after our cats and we forgot to tell him about the contents of the jar. The result was that when we came home we discovered that he had thrown it away because he thought it was something nasty rotting in the refrigerator. Two weeks ago I found an advert in the paper encouraging its readers to buy bottles of kefir. The advert read:

Fancy a drink which will keep you forever young? The latest wellness drink is a milk-based product that contains friendly bacteria and yeasts. It has been in the Caucasus for hundreds of years and is held to be the reason for longevity of its inhabitants.

It costs about $4 a litre.

I think it is time I went down the road from where I now live, to the convent, to collect a bit of the culture, which they were given 25 years ago.

Why pay for what you can have free as long as you keep on giving it away?

He who has ears to hear, let him hear.

Putting Prayer into Perspective

Originally published in: *For Health and Healing.*
The Magazine of the Guild of Health
January 1963

Do you feel guilty when you take a holiday? When you sit down and watch the television, do you think you ought to be doing something? Are you so busy that there's no time to think? Perhaps you are not, but there are plenty of people who are today, and we find them just as much within the Church as outside.

But it's all wrong - we must have our holiday, our relaxation and our withdrawal from everyday life and work. This is not simply because it is good to have a rest, nor because without it we would collapse. There is, rather, a great spiritual principle at work. *Come with me, by yourselves, to some lonely place where you can rest quietly,*[1] says Jesus. Not to escape from the world, nor simply to have a rest from it, but so that we can go back to the world with greater power and insight. So that we can live better and be MORE INVOLVED in the world.

The Provost of Southwark[2] has for years been drawing our attention to the importance of 'Coming and Going', of coming to God, coming to Church in order to go out again, and get on with the job of Christian living in the world. We see the same principle at work with the Iona Community.[3] The Founder, Dr George McLeod, became so concerned with the failure of the Church and with the desperate living conditions in Govan during the thirties, that he left Glasgow for the holy Isle of Iona. As a result of this withdrawal there has come a deeper involvement and a great renewal of the Church's mission.

And again in the comparatively new venture of Voluntary Service Overseas (V.S.O.) the same thing is happening. People are leaving England to work in underdeveloped countries for a year, withdrawn from home, and on returning they see England in clearer perspective. In the end V.S.O. may be of more benefit to England than to the countries in which the volunteers serve.

It is vital for us to withdraw from our daily life and routine and ask ourselves what we are doing and why. It is only when we can stop to think that we see the situation clearly. While we are working and busy, we can't. A cog in a machine cannot see the whole machine. The trouble

---

1. St. Mark, 6: v. 31
2. *The Parish Comes Alive*, E. W. Southcott. (1967)
3. *The Iona Community Story*, T R. Morton (1957)

is that we are very reluctant to withdraw, the Church is reluctant to do it, and so are most groups of people (for instance the political parties). So we have to have the Angry men, the critics of society like John Osborne, to do for society what it refuses to do for itself. The social critics can do this just because they are not accepted by society or they have rejected it.

But we should be prepared to do this for ourselves, and it is part of the purpose of prayer, of retreat, of quiet and of sitting down and doing nothing, to enable us to look at the hard facts about ourselves and the world we live in. We will see the world far more clearly when we look at it from inside the Church, and we see the Church more clearly when we look at it from our place in the world. We will see ourselves more clearly when we look at God, and God more clearly from our knowledge of ourselves.

It is vital in our living to be both involved - in our work, in our life - and also to be withdrawn. This doesn't mean that we don't enter wholeheartedly into our living, far from it. We commit ourselves totally to involvement in the world, simply because we commit ourselves to withdrawal from it. It is all the same thing, so Paul Tillich points out that participation is 'being a part of something from which one is, at the same time separated'.[4] Whatever we are doing loses purpose and direction unless we are both involved and withdrawn.

We must see all our prayer in this context. There is a very real danger of prayer becoming an escape rather than a withdrawal. If we are facing a problem, if we are full of sorrow, if we find life too much for us, there is a great temptation to 'escape' into prayer.

Consequently, it ceases to be prayer; it is simply a form of self-satisfaction, rather than an inspiration for living. Jesus did not go out to pray in order to run away from life: he spent the last night of his earthly life praying in order to come back to face the stark reality of the Crucifixion.

Prayer is not simply for the 'good of our souls', but rather to drive us into more committed living. Our Church-going can be equally as dangerous: it can be a drug to prevent us from being involved in the affairs of the world. We can simply dabble about in so-called 'holy things' rather than being pushed back to live out our Christianity amid all the complications of life. Withdrawal without involvement is mere escapism.

But our withdrawal is also involvement. In real prayer we become withdrawn from the world but involved with God. It is in fact

---

4. *The Courage to Be*, P. Tillich (2000, 2nd ed.)

the same thing. There is no real involvement without withdrawal and no withdrawal without involvement. For wherever we turn, there is God uniting all things in Himself and calling us to Himself by our activity and passivity. If we are too busy to pray our work becomes useless: if our prayer prevents us from activity our prayer is escapism.

What does this mean in practical terms? As individuals it means that we must be involved in prayer, quiet and retreat, but that if this is real prayer it will drive us back into activity. If we are praying for the healing of someone, we will also be doing all we can to help and relieve the sick. Although our activity may be just more prayer. We will see the need in life to bring our 'aloneness'[5] into the company of others, which shows us the value of being alone. Without being alone we will have nothing to give to others. But those who are too much alone we will try to bring into the company of others.

For the local congregation it will mean that there will be plenty of time for prayer and the encouragement of retreats and quiet. The congregation will also take a good look at the local community. The Church would be well advised to be involved in far more prayer and study than is common, before starting some new activity. Parish priests would do well to discover what people are doing, how they live and what they think about, before trying to minister or preach to them. Sociology ought to have a vital part in the life of the Church. If this was done the prayer of the Church would be more relevant because it would be better informed, and consequently more effective. There is also the reverse side to this. What those outside the Church say and think about it becomes very important, and should be listened to and acted upon by the Church. The Church could hardly have a worse public image than it has at the moment, and yet the Church is hardly aware of it, because it takes no notice of what the world is saying. It is withdrawn, too involved in itself.

There is also a message for all those outside the Church. If it could be shown to them that prayer, worship, and retreat - involvement with God - is not simply a means of escape but a means of deeper involvement in the world: if it is seen that Church going is a vital part of work, that prayer is a part of being really busy, that withdrawal leads to involvement; then people might see the practicality of the Christian Gospel. The healing of a sick society cannot begin until the sickness is diagnosed and this diagnosis can only be done from without, from the Godward side. There is a great need for more places of what might

---

5. ibid.

be called centres of 'educative withdrawal'[6] at the local level, where people can become deeply involved by study of the local situation from outside. Also to see what God is saying in the withdrawal, and in the situation. Inspiration for activity could well come from a study of youth, housing conditions, or industrial relations from outside. In such a way the real needs of the world would become apparent, our activities better directed, and the voice of God more clearly heard. We might then have a God's eye view of the situation facing us, and prayer could take its proper place in society and individual lives.

---

6. See D. Bonhoeffer's comments in *Life Together*, Chapter 3(1954)

I Believe
Sermon given at St Andrew's, Headington
11 July 1976

What do we mean when we say 'I Believe?'

It is this question which shows the problem we face when we say the Creed. There was that terrible song some years ago entitled-

> I believe.
> For every drop of rain that falls a flower grows, That someone in the great somewhere will still be there, etc., etc.,

In that connotation 'I believe' basically means a romantic commitment to nonsense; some think the Creed is like that. For others to believe is to accept a series of statements which are necessary for faith. 'Unless you believe this, this and this, then you cannot be a Christian'. Here are a series of propositions you must accept. This is not what belief is either, for we human beings do not like a set of propositions imposed upon us - we will rebel against this in one way or another.

No, our faith is not in a set of propositions; it is in God and all of us know that God is so great and so good and so big that whatever we say about him cannot possibly be adequate. Moreover, if we are honest about ourselves and the world we know that there are many contradictions in life which make certainty in this area very difficult.

If God is good, why is there evil in the world? We cannot be without doubt. Those who seek certainty, those who seek a faith that has all the answers, are seeking a false security: they are running away from reality. No, faith is not accepting untenable propositions. Faith and doubt go together.

Let us look at it another way. To say 'I believe' is not the same as saying 'I know'. To say I know is to have absolute certainty - to say that it can all be proved. But God could never allow us to know Him in that sort of a way. For if there was certainty then there would be no compulsion. If we knew there was a God in the same way we know that two plus two equal four then we should have no choice, and if we had no choice we would have no freedom, and if we had no freedom we could have no love, because love cannot be compelled.

8

So faith which leads to love cannot be based on compulsion but on risk, and on freedom. To say 'I believe' is not to say 'I know' but to say that all the doubts here is a risk worth taking.

For belief is not basically in a set of propositions which make up the Creed but in a person - in Jesus Christ who reveals to us the person of God. Faith is a gift to encounter and be encountered in Christ. To say 'I believe' is to embark on a journey of discovery into God.

The Creeds are not the Gospel - they are as we saw last time, formulas made up by the Church. Jesus did not express himself in doctrines. He did not do so, as Dr. Quick has pointed out because he knew 'that the truths which men live must be formulated and expressed by the inward travail of men's own hearts and minds'.[7]

The Creeds are the answer of one age to faith in Christ, and we respect them as that, but they call us to do the same ourselves, and try and re-formulate them for ourselves. But this we can do only through our own encounter with the Christ of the Gospels, and our common life in Him. That is why the search for new expressions of the faith is an essential part of Christian living. For most of us this will not be in theological formula - but in asking ourselves what is the best way to express our faith in life and in the world today.

But just because faith is not knowledge, and because faith and doubt go together, that expression can never be authoritarian and arrogant. To say 'I believe' expresses a humility before the mystery of God. What this means was well expressed by Dr. Albert Schweitzer who once described his experience in preparing young people for Confirmation when he was a Lutheran pastor in Germany. Many of his fellow pastors in their teaching gave an authoritarian view of the Christian faith as providing all the answers in life. Schweitzer taught us that it explained very little, except the faith to risk all in following Christ. Then came the First World War and on the whole, said Schweitzer, those who were taught that Christianity had the answers came back from the trenches having rejected Christianity. Those who had learned of the risk of faith remained practising Christians. For faith lies not in providing answers, but in living with questions.

To say 'I believe' is more exciting than to say 'I know'. It is a call to a pilgrimage - to an adventure - to a long journey, but one where we risk all to follow Christ.

7. p. 7, Quick, O.C. (1938) *Doctrines of the Creed: Their Basis in Scripture and Their Meaning To-day.* London: Nisbet

The new Doctrine Commission Report[8] begins with these words:

Christian life is an adventure, a voyage of discovery, a journey, sustained by faith and hope, towards a final and complete communion with the Love at the heart of all things. There are times in this life when the Christian finds in himself an ever deepening confidence which, even if it does not draw the sting of pain, difficulty or sorrow, yet enables him to pass victoriously through them. This confidence brings with it an inner conviction, so strong that it can feel very like actual knowledge, about the reality of his goal and the rightness of his way. Life is not a puzzle of trying to find out whether the goal exists, and how to get to it if it does; it is an experience of being drawn by a love which most certainly does exist, and which by the power of its influence at any given moment confirms the right way towards itself. But equally, at the other extreme, there are times when there is no sense of being drawn, no directing influence is felt, conviction can give place not just to doubt but to active scepticism, and life may seem futile, cruel and overwhelming. Most of one's life, no doubt, is spent in the unexciting middle zone, neither powerfully drawn nor totally desolate. But to be a Christian means that, whatever one's state, the journey goes on. It is staking everything on the belief that this way of using our one and only life will in the end be validated not only as the best for our human condition but as most truly in accord with ultimate reality.

Let us launch out on that journey now.

8. Doctrine Commission (1976): *Christian believing: the nature of the Christian faith and its expression in Holy Scripture and creeds*, London:SPCK

On Dispensing with Pews
A discussion paper for the PCC of St Andrew's, Headington
1977

The suggestion that pews should be removed and replaced by chairs is, as Maguire and Murray[9] point out in their report, an aspect of the reversion to the medieval pattern of Church design. It cannot be regarded as an innovation. It does have considerable advantages and I intend in this paper to try and point them out so we can think them through.

As an aid to worship
We have discovered over the last four years the great advantages in having a flexible chancel where everything is moveable. Thus for different purposes we have been able to use the chancel in different ways. We are wrong to think that there is only one way to worship and the great value of people being able to see each other, speak to each other and move around is very great. What we have found for small numbers in the chancel would be equally true for larger numbers in the body of the Church.

Worship is essentially a community activity and to sit in rows looking at the back of people's necks all the time does not create a community spirit.

While we would not want to re-order the Church all the time, there are occasions when the present arrangement is highly unsatisfactory. This is especially true when we have large numbers of children. Those sitting in the north aisle can neither see nor hear anything when the clergy are in the chancel. The opportunity to worship 'in the round' on occasion must not be ignored. Similarly, the use of more flexible seating would be a help when we are not expecting large numbers but when the chancel is too small and something in between is needed.

Moreover, as experimental worship develops, the opportunity to have more space for movement is important.
Already we are in great difficulty when we have a choir, or need to put a special group somewhere, because we have to move the pews - which is a heavy and backbreaking business. Chairs would be easier and more efficient. Worship requires flexibility. At the same time the size of our congregation means that we must not lose any seating capacity.

---

9. Maguire & Murray were consultant architects for the restoration project at St. Andrew's Church.

Aesthetic considerations

Maguire and Murray have pointed out the great value of more space. Photographs of the Church before they worked on it in 1960 show that what they did then has brought out the good features of the building. Their present proposals take this further. There are here questions of taste and judgement which are not easy to assess, and that is why we are very fortunate to have the advice of some of the leading Church architects in this country.

Look at any Church without pews and you will see immediately how the building is given a sense of height and space, because the pillars are exposed and not cut off half way down.

Practical considerations

Parts of the report are a direct response to the last quinquennial inspection which we are bound to implement. We do have to redecorate and we do have to deal with the lighting. It is true that neither the floor nor the pews are in that quinquennial inspection but we launched the appeal on the understanding we would do our best to put the Church in really good order for the future. The wood block floor is becoming dangerously loose and some blocks have rot in them. The last survey did notice furniture beetle in some of the pews and those whose ends rest on the outside walls are already rotting at these ends. While they will last some time their days are certainly numbered. We might be advised to dispose of them while we can get something for them, rather than wait until they disintegrate.

The Stewardship argument

This point is central to the whole debate. If our appeal is fully successful we shall be able to have a church which is not going to be a drain on resources in the future. This will set free more of our money for other purposes. But we must also exercise stewardship of our buildings.

It is surely not right for us to maintain a building, however beautiful, which is only used for about 12 hours a week and also a Parish Hall which is underused as well. At the public meeting in June 1976, the general conclusion was that while people were not sure about the Church being used for any or every function, the removal of the pews to create space in different ways would be worth considering. The matter of using it more widely could not arise until people felt happy about it and it became clear that we did not wish to maintain both the Parish Church and the Parish Hall. We are not considering the disposal of the Parish Hall at this time.

The question is therefore about how we can effectively use the Church more fully within these guidelines. The Church does not belong to the people who happen to worship in it - it belongs to the whole community. While the rights of worshippers must always be preserved, the whole community should have a say in how it is used. The way in which we use the building is an expression of what we believe about the Gospel. Is it something to keep to ourselves or is it something we wish to share with everyone? To keep it to ourselves would be a denial of the Gospel we profess to believe in. While the Church is full of pews both forms of worship and any other activity is severely curtailed. We must remember that we live in a missionary situation. Smug, selfish religion is not what Christianity is about and it must not be what our building is about.

The changing situation in the Parish

We have to look to the future. We are witnessing in this parish a minor social revolution with implications which are hard to grasp. We are becoming urban, with large numbers of people working, but not living, in our midst. In what ways can the Church respond to this new situation? It is not clear but we may be in a position to offer some facilities for worship and for cultural activities which will not otherwise be available in this area. The coming festival will be a good taste of what is possible.

What is a sacred building?

There is a great deal which could be said here and those who wish to consider it fully should read The Secular Use of Church Buildings by Professor J.G. Davies. At this point I would just like to quote from Fr. Walbert Buhlmann, a leading Roman Catholic missionary in Africa who is concerned about the role of the Church in mission in the modern world:

That we have come to regard as natural and unquestionable turns out to be no more than a phenomenon of history (recent history at that) which finds no support in the Gospel. In Judaism and in all pre- Christian religions, the sacred was a central concept: it could be a particular place or person set apart for the divine, holy, powerful, associated with

13

reverence, fear and taboo. But Christ desacralized the domain for the sacred or, better, he sanctified the whole world and all man. No longer only in the temple, or on this or that hill, but in every place will the Father be worshipped in spirit and in truth. The temple is replaced by the person of Christ, for here is one greater than the temple and by the congregation, the people of God. The apostles drew further inferences. 'We are the temple of the living God' - 'Let yourselves be built up as living stones into a spiritual temple'. Consequently, Christians built no temple, but assembled in their own houses, then in community buildings and finally in basilicas designed as assembly places. Gradually, the tendency towards desacralizing grew. But even in the middle ages the Church of the people of God was often available for all purposes and not just for worship: for the agape, for trials, for political assemblies and for markets. Until 200 years ago, churches were nearly always multi-purpose buildings, in which the whole life of the congregation was played out. Only since then has worship and the rest of the life of the congregation been separated. This is not an ideal; it is rather a warning sign.

Nowadays, instead of churches designed exclusively for worship, we are beginning to build community centres where the Christian Community can again be found with all its pre-occupations, hopes and activities. At the heart of it all, and as the climax, is the Sunday celebration of the Eucharist. It is an idea that should spread in the Third Church. How can we use foreign money to build churches in poor countries to be used only on Sunday mornings and then a few years later, write to another address to finance a parish hall which will be used a few evenings in the week? No institution in the world could allow its resources to be so badly utilised as the Church. We should, therefore, plan buildings for more than one purpose especially in the country and the outskirts of cities. I would even go as far to say that it could be a sin against the Church to build a church.

(*The Coming of the Third Church* by W. Buhlmann)

What then would the Church be used for?

This is where people's anxieties come to a head. What are we suggesting? Two points should perhaps be made:

• Nothing will happen in the Church which the PCC does not approve of. Decisions in this area must be made by the PCC.

• It is most likely that nothing will happen that has not

already happened. Thus the churches over recent years have been used for concerts (handbell ringers, singers, Salvation Army Band for example), flower festivals and exhibitions, talks and public meetings, drama and discussion groups.

All these things have already happened. We also serve coffee in Church every Sunday. I cannot see that we should need to extend this list at all - but with chairs rather than pews we could do them more efficiently, effectively and with much more comfort.

Conclusion

I do hope we will not make too much of this issue. It is really a simple matter of creating space and flexibility in the use of the Church building. I realise that people have anxieties and I hope they will express them clearly and publicly. This paper will be duplicated so that people can act more fully and the architect's report is also available. I remain to be convinced that there are strong arguments against those expressed here. I think that at the end of the day we are dealing with emotions, feelings and faith here rather than with intellectual argument and all this must be openly expressed. I know it will sound prejudiced but it expresses my own feelings if I say that the choice seems to be between having pews to feel safe in and to keep my faith to myself, or of creating space to BE, providing flexibility in action which removes the security but allows us to make the experiments and take the risks that faith is made of.

Whitsunday 1977

Christian Dialogue in the Age of Mission

The People Next Door: Regional Training Conference[10]
1968

'The age of Missions is at an end; the age of Mission has begun, - so Bishop Stephen Neill describes the present state of the History of the Christian Missions. The task of the Church has been the same in every age - to serve God's mission; to be the sending Church of a sending God; to witness the redemptive work of God in Christ in the world which he loves. But now, 'the age of Missions is at an end.'[11] Stephen Neill says what he means by this - the time is now past when some Churches sent missionaries and missions to heathen lands. The Church now exists in every country (it may not be very large - but it exists). The Christian Presence is there to witness to Christ in every society. In a world which is now one world - an interdependent technological world - God's mission is to be carried on, in all six continents.

The age of Missions is at an end - we can now see more clearly that mission is the function of the whole Church and of every Christian - this is what we mean when we say we believe in an 'Apostolic Church'. For mission is not simply a geographical matter - mission is to be in depth as well as in breadth. There are over 200 million people in the world who have never heard the name of Christ and that number increases daily; there are millions more even among those who call themselves Christians who need a deeper commitment to Christ, and a deeper participation in God's mission. The age of Mission has begun - every Christian is called to be a missionary wherever he is, whatever he does.[12]

What then is a missionary? A missionary is a man who crosses frontiers, who goes out from where he is, across a frontier to others. For some this frontier is still a geographical one; but in this one world this is not so significant. There are many other frontiers to cross; political, racial, cultural, social, industrial frontiers. For one of the features of this secularized society is that there are many more barriers, many smaller societies of like-minded people, who rarely cross the frontiers into others. The Christian responsibility is to do so. (So some regard the Freedom Movement in America as one of the most significant missionary

---

10. 'The People Next Door' was an ecumenical study programme organised by the British Council of Churches which began in 1967.
11. Neill, S. (1964) *A History of Christian Missions, (The Pelican History of the Church, Vol. 6)*, London: Pelican
12. Editors' note: Despite the unfortunately gendered language in this article, we have chosen to retain it as it reflects the prevailing writing style of the time.

activities of our age). This seems to me to be the core of the message of the Mexico Conference of the DWME (The Division on World Mission and Evangelism) to the Churches.

The missionary today is therefore the Christian of every place, who crosses the frontier with Christ to bear witness to him. It seems to me that a valuable way of looking at the role of mission is in terms of Dialogue. The problem is that Churches have neglected their apostolic role. A recent conference which met to consider the mission of the Church in West Africa commented as follows:

> The tragedy of the Church is that there are many Churches fully and faithfully proclaiming the Gospel to themselves.[13]

The Churches, not only in West Africa, are busy talking to themselves, involved in monologue and not dialogue. It is that dialogue with the world - across the frontiers, which we will consider now. I wish to put before you a series of principles of dialogue, which may be a guide to the idea of mission as dialogue.

1. A common basis

The basis of our dialogue with others is our common humanity. In affirming this, the Christian is affirming the doctrine of creation. But the Christian responsibility goes further than this; Christians need to share with all their brothers what they have found to be meaningful for them. We can see that the discussion on the basis   of common humanity between Christians and Communists in such bodies as the Christian Peace Conference of Prague. There is a need recognized both by Christians and Marxists to gain a clearer view of the world today. Both are seeking to set people free from economic, social and political domination and alienation. This should lead to a new openness on both sides, so that Christians may recognise the humanitarian perspective of Marxism and the Marxists may be able to understand and recognise the religious aspect of life as influencing history. This is already happening as Communists in Russia investigate the cultural roots of Russian society and find them to be Christian.

While many of the new nations are seeking to find a firm basis, a Christian concern for the nature and destiny of man shared with all men of whatever conviction, us a vital part of the Christian mission. Thus the Christian Dialogue may well not begin on a religious basis

---

13. Source unknown

or a religious subject, but on those matters of common concern to which there may be no clear answers, but on which the Christian doctrine of man may cast some light.

2. A self-understanding

But for this the Christian requires a real understanding of his own position. He needs to understand himself in relation to Christ. He needs to understand his own acceptance by Christ. He needs, above all, to be aware of what the Gospel is all about. There seems to be a real danger at the moment in avoiding the question of what the Gospel is in favour of talking about - structures, renewal, liturgy and so on. But we need to be aware here that we share a common basis with others – non-Christians – a common basis which lies in faith and not knowledge. What we differ about is our interpretation of life – our faith.

But self-understanding must also lead us to see ourselves under the judgement of God. God's judgement on our failure to enter into dialogue, in our failure to communicate. So the Study Centre for the Study of Buddhism in Ceylon is commenting on the fact of Resurgent Buddhism today, while seeing that it was in part due to nationalism and the adoption of the methods of Christian mission, see that the main cause lies in the failure of the Church. Resurgent Buddhism was God's judgement on the Churches because:

a. There had been no Christian social witness.
b. Christianity had been too identified with the West.
c. The failure of the Church to speak across the Communist / non-Communist frontier.
d. The Churches' excessive dogmatism.

So also the East German theologian Helmut Gollwitzer sees that the Church has itself been the cause of the growth of communism. He writes as follows: 'Experience of the un-Christian nature of the Christian congregation has contributed to the growth of communist messianism.'[14]

He therefore argues that the prerequisite for effective dialogue by the Churches is to give real evidence of deep repentance for their own failure. Self-understanding leading to repentance is necessary for dialogue.

---

14. Gollwitzer, H. (1970) *The Christian Faith and the Marxist Criticism of Religion.* [Eds: For further discussion of Golwitzer's legacy, see McMaken (2013)].

3. Real understanding of the other person's position

The great missionaries of the past have been those who have taken the time and trouble to understand the language, culture and way of life of those to whom they have gone with the Gospel. Matteo Ricci, Di Nobili, Hudson Taylor and so on. They took the time, a long time, to understand the world into which they went. They were not concerned with immediate conversion but with a long-term policy based on Christian understanding of the people.

Many have taken this further to seeing Christ in those to whom they talked. For as the EACC[15] has commented: 'The Christian approaches dialogue with a concept of man which includes not only judgement of men in their sin but also their standing within the saving action of God.'

Some like Fr. Pannikkar in *The Unknown Christ of Hinduism* (1964) regard Hinduism as Christianity in potency. For Christ sums up all men and all things in himself. The role of mission is to reveal the Christ who is already there.

Secondly, such understanding will save the Church from the terrible blemishes, which have marred so much of the history of missions. The intolerant and uncomprehending attitude of missionaries to social customs especially in relation to polygamy, the bride price and role of women were due to failure to understand the nature of society (e.g. Roland Allen[16]).

4. A common language

There can be no dialogue unless we understand what we are saying to each other. Nor is it simply a matter of learning a new language. This raises the whole question of Indigenisation. Many of the strange sects which have arisen in Africa and Asia have done so because the traditional Christian Churches do not express the Christian Faith in the thought forms and culture of the people. Is this not also one of the reasons why Christianity does not speak to this generation in this land? Because it expresses itself in out-of-date thought forms and language? Mission, says Bengt Sundkler,[17] is translation. The Christian Gospel has to be translated. It was because it was translated from Hebrew into Greek thought forms that it took root in the 1st century world. The process of translation must continue. It is a dangerous and risky process, but so is mission - so is the way of the Cross.

---

15. East Asia Christian Conference, founded in 1957 [Eds: later renamed CCA: Christian Conference of Asia; for further discussion of this see Poon (2011)]

16. [Eds: See Payne, J.D. (2003) 'The Legacy of Roland Allen']

17. Sundkler, B. G.M. (1960) *The Christian Ministry in Africa*, London: SCM Press

5. Honesty and openness

True dialogue, based upon our common humanity, should lead to complete honesty and openness to each other. It should mean that Christians are prepared openly to admit their failures and mistakes. For we are all under the judgement of God and the open acknowledgement of failure is part of the proclamation of the Gospel. This is again a very costly thing; true dialogue takes time; it may be some time before people feel free to say what they really want. It will hurt, it may mean rejection at times but it is the way to true communication and understanding. Too often we avoid realism - it costs too much. But Jesus Christ is the truth and we must seek the truth at all costs.

6. Awareness of the risk involved

What I have already said should be enough. Dialogue is a costly thing - it will test our faith. But we should expect it to. Part of the costliness will be that of listening; listening to Christ speaking to us in others. We need much more to be a listening Church.

7. A willingness to change

The dialogue which Jesus had with the Jewish Authorities ended in crucifixion because they were not prepared to change. Not prepared to change their ideas about God, not prepared to change their way of life, not prepared to change their thought forms. If the missionary is the one who crosses frontiers, then he must be prepared to change. He must change his way of life, he must change his friends, he must change his scale of values, his cultural background, his political allegiance, and all this will be very costly. To refuse to change is to have an unbiblical approach to God, for the God of the Bible is dynamic and not static.

8. Demonstrate what we say in action

One of the reasons why Christianity is not taken seriously is because in this pragmatic age people do not see what Christianity means in practice. Christians seem to be no better and sometimes worse than other people. In the new nations an inherited colonial attitude sometimes stays with the Christians which makes them seem to be the enemies of the new nation. But it goes deeper than this; God's love to man needs to show itself in action. So the EACC has commented:

> The disposition of God towards men in Jesus Christ cannot in the last
> analysis, be communicated apart from a life which makes it credible. It
> must be demonstrated by those who bear his name.

Mission has done much in this direction. The great emphasis on education has been the basis of much of the modern world of today. Not least in terms of the setting up of new independent nations in Africa and Asia. So while the cynic sometimes says "the Christians come to our lands with the Bible in their hands; before we knew what had happened we had the Bible and they had our lands", others would echo the words of the imprisoned S. Rhodesian nationalist leader, the Rev. N. Sithole when he wrote: 'The missionary came in time and laid explosives under colonialism. The Bible is now doing what we could not do with our spears.'[18]

The emphasis on the individual in the 19th Century has produced the political leaders of Africa and Asia of today.

This action must continue. But to the African and Asian the so-called Christian countries of the West do not seem to be showing much Christian love and service to the rest of the world. This is the age of partnership, but what partnership is being shown by the West when it uses up 75% of the world's wealth on itself and over 50% of the world's population has only 18% of the world's wealth? As long as this state of affairs continues it is hardly likely that the new nations will have much time for the Christian Faith. Love and service in action is not just a fruit of the Christian Mission. It is mission itself and the Christian Gospel is meaningless without it.

9. Common activity

Dialogue without action is only partial; we come to under- stand each other by sharing in common activity. Therefore, the Church should not deplore the taking over of part of the things it started, e.g. schools and hospitals, by the new nations; it should rejoice at it.

For in taking over these things they are acknowledging their value and implicitly accepting the Christian principles which led to their original foundation. Partnership and sharing are essential parts of dialogue. We should expect this to be the new way of Christian Mission; by sharing and serving the State. Such is the pattern of mission now developing in Port Harcourt in Eastern Nigeria, where Christians of many denominations are working together with the State in helping to deal with a massive social problem (Trade Unions., Schools, Youth, Workers' Education Association, Health, etc.).

Our common Humanity under God should lead us to co-operate with all men who are seeking to build up mankind into that

---

18. [Eds: for a more contemporary take on these issues, see Etherington, N. (ed) (2005) *Missions and Empire*: Oxford: Oxford University Press]

21

freedom which is God's will for all. So Christians in Eastern Germany see it as part of their Christian obligation to share in the responsibility which all have in common, whether Christian or not, to organize and sustain the life of the nation. (Such is the interpretation of Romans 13 - see *Pro-Existence* by E. Adler[19]). Whatever the Communist may do, says H. Gollwitzer, the Christian realises that it cannot be final. So he writes:

> [The Christian] is therefore assured that man's decision to reject God is ultimately powerless in face of God's decision for man. The Christian in the world is the witness and messenger of God's decision.

So the Christian needs to co-operate with all men and fulfil his mission which is to affirm God's decision for man.

10. Personal encounter

Dialogue involves meeting; it requires the face-to-face encounter of people. There can be no substitute for personal encounter in the Christian Mission. On the basis of our common humanity, our common sharing of the same problems and difficulties, our common need to listen to Christ speaking to us through each other and our common need to understand and adapt to each other we can bear witness to God's decision for man by the costly acceptance of the other in personal encounter. In this age of Mission we need to realise that it is not our mission, but God's, and therefore it is not a matter of the Christian offering the full Gospel to the unbeliever, but a matter of Dialogue. It is a matter of sharing, a partnership under God, listening to Him and affirming his decision for man in Christ.

The People Next Door is, among other things, an exercise in Christian Dialogue. It will therefore involve the above principles.

We may sum them up in the Parable of the Good Samaritan. Here Jesus tells how the Samaritan crossed the frontier (he was unacceptable) and came to the traveller 'where he was'. This is the basis of dialogue because it is the basis of the Incarnation. We come to people 'where they are' in every sense of that. We do so because of the finality of God's decision for man; this is the cornerstone of our faith in Jesus Christ, Emmanuel, GOD WITH US.

---

19. Adler, E , & Seiffert, L (eds.) *'Pro-Existence': Christian Voices in East Germany 1954 – 1963*, London: SCM Press

People on the Move
Sermon given at Keele University[20]
February 1985

Hebrews 12: vv. 1 - 2:
With all these witnesses to Faith around us like a cloud we must throw off every encumbrance, every sin to which we cling, and run with resolution the race for which we are entered, our eyes fixed on Jesus on whom Faith depends start to finish.

Christians are people on the move. Whenever they become fixed and static in mind, worship or in lifestyle, then questions need to be asked. Christians are people on the move, because Jesus Christ is ever before them leading them to new effort, to new pastures, to new risks of Faith.

Such is the picture the writer to the Hebrews gives us - Jesus is the pioneer, blazing the trail before us to God, so that where he is we might be also.

Christians are people on the move; that was what Vatican II was on about when it described the Church as the Pilgrim People:

The Church like a pilgrim in a foreign land presses forward amid the persecutions of the world and the consolation of God, announcing the Cross and death of the Lord until he comes.[21]

Thus also John Vincent has described Jesus as a sort of Pied Piper. Jesus, he says, 'is homeless because he must always be on the move.' Jesus and his Disciples, he says, 'fit into the category of vagrants' and so he writes:

Jesus' Movement is a Movement designed to prepare people and the world itself to act in the light of the Kingdom of God. We do not see the Kingdom, acquire it, build it, or enjoy it. What we do is to join a Movement which looks for it, acts as if it already existed, takes hold of its final reality and embodies bits of it now.[22]

Now the Ecumenical Movement is part of that process and the concept of Local Ecumenical Projects is one way in which people can

20. Keele University Chaplaincy was a pioneering ecumenical experiment, founded in 1965, with shared services and shared ministry between different Christian denominations
21. *Lumen Gentium*, 1964. See also Küng, H. (2001, new ed.) *The Church*, London: Bloomsbury
22. Eds: exact source unknown. See Vincent (1969), also Shannahan (2016)

23

grasp and act in relation to the Kingdom of God. But it is not always seen that way. Too often it is not seen like that. Too much Ecumenism has become petty and small-minded with a very narrow vision of what might be done or can be done.

I remember very many years ago talking to Archdeacon George Youell about the plans for Keele - about the hopes and expectancies of the Keele Chaplaincy as a sign and a pointer to a greater Unity. Keele, as befits it as a University, led the way, set the scene, and began a process.

The early development of what were called 'Areas of Ecumenical Experiment' came after the Nottingham Faith and Order Conference of 1964 and were days of ecumenical expectancy and euphoria. Alas, much steam has gone out of the ecumenical boat since then. The ecumenical seashore is covered with wrecks of failed Union Schemes, ineffective Councils of Churches and empty hopes. This is not the time to examine the causes of this failure. Suffice it say that it comes from a strange mixture of lack of faith, naive planning and unrealistic expectations. But many have been hurt and pained by the process, are a little chary of starting again, and will eye the new B.C.C.[23] Initiative with much caution.

But through all the comings and goings of National Ecumenism, there has been a steady growth in the number of places where local Ecumenism has become more than a token, where united congregations have indeed become signs of the Kingdom; where there is new life and new hope. These vary – the *Sharing of Church Buildings Act*[24] has followed a sharing of resources and a growing congregational life.

Local Covenants have enabled Churches to plan a common strategy in Mission. Shared Ministries are growing in confidence. The processes have involved much learning. We now have much experience in the ways in which such local Ecumenism may be enabled and sustained and this is the point of this occasion:

- to renew commitment;
- to establish a pattern which will ensure an ongoing
- growth in ecumenical relations;
- to look to the future with growing confidence.

But let us do so not with small ideas but with big ones. Let us remember that we are a people on the move. The Son of Man has nowhere to lay his head. As soon as we become smug and settled we shall see that our Lord has moved on ahead. Can our text give us some clues about the way we may approach this?

---

23. British Council of Churches
24. https://ctbi.org.uk/sharing-church-buildings-act-1969/ (accessed 29.05.17)

Clouds of witnesses - we are never alone; there is a growing band of people who have experienced the joy and deepness of ecumenical living and worship and who do not wish to go back. In our mobile Society, not least in a University Campus, people are coming and going - so a new Church is emerging - one which will not accept the narrowness of Denominationalism. One which sees the true diversity and a greater richness of the Gospel than we have ever seen before.

Throw off every encumbrance: if we really are on the move we need to determine what is necessary and what is unnecessary baggage. This is no easy task; at the heart of it lies the current Doctrinal Debate. In seeking a common life and Faith we have to see what Faith is, what is essential and what is not. Here Christians will differ greatly, but the way must also be the way of the Gospel, fulfilled not with acrimony but in the Spirit of Love, acceptance and reconciliation. If we can do that we may grow greatly through this task.

Casting off every sin: every clinging to ourselves and our own identity. There is a real sense in which the Ecumenical Movement is a Call to see whether we believe the Gospel we preach, and that Gospel speaks that whoever would save his life must lose it. Only if we are willing to cast off what we cling to can we come into the Kingdom of God.

Run with resolution looking to Jesus: we must count the cost. To look to Jesus is to go his way and be imitators of him. That means paying the price, for the way of Christ is costly. One of the chief reasons for ecumenical failure lies just here; we want things to be easy and comfortable. The way of Christ is never thus. The test of Faith is not how successful we are; not how many people we attract; not how articulate we are about Faith - there is one test: how close we are to the Crucified Christ; how closely we suffer with him.

"When you go to Heaven", said Pope John XXIII, "the Lord will not judge you as to whether you have achieved Unity but whether you have worked for Unity and suffered for Unity."

For the Church is ever before us. Total Unity lies only in him. We can but follow, and we can but obey. May we all this evening, as we commit ourselves afresh, look to Jesus the Author and Perfector of our Faith; who for the sake of the joy that lay ahead of him: *endured the Cross, making light of its disgrace, and has taken his seat at the right hand of the throne of God.*[25]

---

25. Hebrews 12: 2

Keys

Farewell Sermon given at St Bartholemew's, Tong
June 21st 1987

Matthew 19: v.19:
I will give you the keys of the Kingdom of Heaven.

Here in this church, in the original stained glass, St. Peter is depicted as he is also on Sir Richard Vernon's Tomb as holding the keys. A symbol which goes back to this passage in St. Matthew's Gospel - a much disputed passage used by many to justify the primacy of Peter in the Church; but look at the passage carefully. It is about Peter - but it is also about the rest of the disciples; it is not about the Church - it is about the Kingdom of Heaven; the place where God rules.

Where does the imagery of Keys come from here? It takes us back to the Old Testament to Isaiah 22 v. 22 where it is spoken of Eliakim - the Steward-elect of the Royal Household. He is replacing Shebna who has not been worthy of the post. *I will place on his shoulder the Key of the House of David - he shall open the doors for others.* That is the real implication of the text.

Now keys are a great part of the life of any Vicar - rarely such interesting keys as those of Tong, with which Ruth and I have been pleased to open and shut this church over the last nine years, but we hope we have been doing it for others, and we hope that we have not been simply opening the doors for people to enter the church, but to catch a vision of something bigger and greater than them, and bigger and greater than the Church; the Kingdom of Heaven - the active rule of God in their hearts and lives, and while we are all very unworthy stewards, we do hope that the doors have been opened a little.

For the moment I would like to look to the future - your future and my future, and to look at it in terms of Keys – of clues about the way ahead.

A key opens things up - that is what the Gospel is about; opening up our closed minds - our preconceived ideas to new and great possibilities. The temptation of the age is to stick to the trusted and the known, but that is to have the idea of a very small God - for God is greater than any of our conceptions of him, so we need opening up, in prayer, in worship, in reflection, to more and more of the greatness and the mystery. Never lose that key.

26

A key - like the key to the wall safe in the Vestry (which doesn't always work!) can show us new treasures - we can ever be learning to appreciate not only the new but the old; discovering more and more of our roots - giving identity and purpose. This is something we have tried to do; treasure it, and keep at it, for God is the God of the past and the future, and we learn of the future from the past. This key is very valuable, and must never be thought to be worthless.

The next key is the Key to the future of the parish. It is not a clergy key but a laity key. If you really do care about the Gospel in this place, then you will not keep it to yourself; you will share it with this changing community; you will go out in love and care to all - and I mean all - not just those of the same social class or the same interests as yourself. The key to the future lies in Lay Ministry.

I never felt during the last few years that the time was right for such a move, but I have known as Archdeacon that I have not been a very good Vicar, that much of the pastoral contact and care has not been sustained because of my other commitments. That will always be the same. You are the people who must visit the sick and the bereaved - you are the people who must prepare the young for Confirmation - you are the people who must prepare couples for marriage and for baptism. You are the ones for whom this ministry of Christ's will be taken forward, and it may well be as Christian Ministry develops in new directions, that you will look around the congregation and say - that's the woman or that's the man whom we would like to be our Vicar - from among our own number. If you really care, that is the key which opens the way ahead. I hope we have laid some tentative foundations - it now needs to go forward.

The fourth and last key is the key of reconciliation. In every community - in every household - there are tensions; there are difficulties - there are conflicts to be overcome. If Christians cannot be reconcilers in the community, they might as well not call themselves Christians. That reconciliation begins with listening, with understanding, with sharing in the lives of others. There is too much which is hidden and not understood; anxieties not revealed lead to prejudice; guilt unresolved leads to anger; pretensions based on false images of ourselves lead to unreality. The only way is an open, loving, caring community, and that is what we are called to be. Real openness based upon an understanding of God's total acceptance of ourselves as we are.

An appreciation of the treasures and mysteries of life and a commitment to a Christian Ministry in which we all share and participate; a Spirit of Love and Reconciliation - these are the Keys of to the Kingdom of Heaven; don't lose them I say to myself and to you, but also don't just leave them lying around - use them, for there are many doors to be opened and Jesus who stands at the door and knocks is on the other side of every one of them.

So I lay down these keys which in a sense are a symbol of Ministry and hand them over, not just to George Frost,[26] but to you all.

We would like to thank you all as a family for your kindness, tolerance, understanding and support over these years, which have been very formative for us, and we wish you Godspeed. You know that Tong will never be far from our hearts and yours.

Pray that those who are Stewards of the Kingdom may use the Keys wisely and open the Kingdom of Heaven to all believers.

---

26. The Ven. George Frost was Bob's successor as Archdeacon of Salop.

Many are called, but few are chosen
Sermon given at SS Mary & John, Cowley
12th October 2014

Matthew 22: v.1-14:
Many are called, but few are chosen

It may be just because I am getting old, but I find many trends in society quite worrying. There is so much around us that turns us in on ourselves and not outwards to the people. People are endlessly on their mobile phones on the internet or on Twitter and Facebook with people we call "friends" whom we have never met. It is very tedious to hear endless conversations people have on their mobile phones, which usually begin with the words "I am on the bus."

I do not possess a mobile phone, both because I don't want to be that available and also because it is an expense I do not need. But I am really concerned that society is turning in on itself instead of outwards to the world around us. We see it in society and in politics with people concentrating on self-interest rather than on the desperate needs of the world around us.

Today's Gospel is a parable about people who are wrapped up in themselves. The King holds a very elaborate banquet and invites many to it, but they turn away. They would rather deal with their own affairs than reach out to others. Or even to their ruler. It is interesting that the example given shows people concerned with their work to the exclusion of anything else. How many of us are like that? Some others, the parable tells us, are even more desperate and so self- centred and sure they are right that they kill the messengers. We are seeing this in intolerant religion at this present time. It is so very easy to be self-obsessed that we are the only people that matter and know we are right and so diminish the value of others. The King is so annoyed he destroys these people.

The servants go out to invite others. These are the neglected, the poor, the homeless and the immigrants. These are the victims of other people's self-obsession. For that is what happens. When we turn in on ourselves, others get excluded and rejected. This is the reverse of our faith which calls us out of ourselves - to be open to God, open to the world and open to other people. Alas, so often, even the Church can turn in on itself. I sometimes think that the Church of England is in danger of becoming 'The Society of Self-Preservation of the Church of England' instead of being open and accepting of the whole world and serving others.

But then the parable has another twist. The King examines the guests to see if they are properly dressed for the occasion. This seems like a contradiction. Someone is removed for not having the proper wedding garment, but from Matthew's point of view to accept the Gospel call means we must understand that there is a price to be paid. The cross has to be taken up. Self-interest has to be rejected.

Now, in saying all this, I am giving this passage a bit of a twist. When Matthew was writing his Gospel, he was writing it for the Jews who had become Christians. The destruction of the original followers is a reference to the Pharisees who reject the gospel. The destruction of the towns refers to the destruction of Jerusalem by the Romans in AD70. The Gospel demonstrates that God accepts Gentiles as well as Jews. A new covenant is being established for all humanity. But even the Jews were meant to accept those who live among them as neighbours and strangers.

Matthew is applying the teaching of Jesus to the community in which he finds himself. And that is what we are called to do. To apply the Gospel to the place where we are and the people we live amongst.

Behind the Passion Narratives
13th February 2013

In looking at the Passion narratives in the Gospels it is very important to understand their origins. The very early Christian Communities, meeting in Houses, had no scriptures except the Old Testament but the stories of Jesus were collected and put together as the Church evolved. These stories were used in early Christian Worship.

Thus the patterns of worship pre-date the Gospels - not the other way round. So behind the Gospels lie both patterns of Worship and lectionaries for the reading of Scripture.

Below I list the dates of the Gospels and to whom they were addressed but it is very important to understands that the way the Gospels came to be written was affected by both the communities to which they were written and the particular theological stance of the Gospel writers.

Thus Matthew writing for an early Christian Jewish Community sees Jesus as the new Moses, so there are close parallels with the Moses stories. Luke, on the other hand, sees Jesus as the new Elijah and emphasises the prophetic nature of his role. John, the more philosophical writer, seems to have a Platonic background where Jesus is the link between humanity (below) and the eternal God (above). Thus the text *You must be born again* actually means 'You must be born from above'– e.g. by God; and *You must be born of water and the spirit* is similar: e.g. by the waters of human birth and the Spirit of God. This is why it is so unwise to take bits from different Passion narratives and put them together (as in the *Seven Words from the Cross*) because it disrupts the integrity of each Gospel writer's individual approach.

Thus when we come to the Passion narratives we have to realise that the choice of biblical passages, like the great emphasis in them derived from Psalm 22, came about because Psalm 22 was used in the early Christian Holy Week worship, which predates the Gospels.

The Gospel of Mark was written around 72 AD (it refers to the destruction of Jerusalem, which took place in 70 AD). So there are about 40 years of Christian worship behind its writing. It may relate to the memories of Peter, and was written in Rome.

Matthew was writing a little later, probably in Jerusalem, and incorporates a lot of Mark's material. It shows the early Church dealing with problems of discipline and the like.

Luke is a two-part work with Acts, and is a little later   than

Matthew; but is expecting the end of the world to come and is addressed to a different community, and infers more settled Christian Communities.

John is quite a bit later (110AD?). No one knows who wrote it and it related to a time when Christians are being persecuted. It has been edited and has at least two endings.

It also needs to be noted that there were many other Gospels which did not get into the canon of Scripture: the New Testament as we know it was not put together until the 5th Century AD.

How often should I forgive?

Sermon at All Saints Church, Highfield 11 September, 2011

Matthew 18: v.21
How often should I forgive?

My normal place of worship for a Sunday is All Saints Convent on St Mary's Road in East Oxford. I normally walk there from where I live, further up the Cowley Road. On my way there I pass a community hall, which is used every Sunday by a Black Church congregation. They are already singing when I walk past at about 10:30 and the service is still going on when I walk back at about 12:30. I can often hear a preacher haranguing the congregation but it is not always easy to hear what is being said. However, not very long ago as I went past, a woman preacher made the following statement: "God does not put a full stop in your life, He always puts a comma."

I thought it was quite a good remark and it came back to me when reading today's passage from St. Matthew's Gospel. We need to know the background of this passage. Matthew, like St Paul before him, was addressing a particular congregation of new Christians. They were mainly people who had converted from Judaism and saw the Church as the New Israel.

But, as with St Paul, the community Matthew was addressing was facing many practical questions about how to organise their life and how to cope with difficult people and situations. The question about discipline in relation to people who broke the rules and who offended other people was complicated. There had to be some form of discipline. How many times should a person be accepted back before they were to be excommunicated from the Christian fellowship? It is in this context that we get the parable of the unforgiving servant. His King forgives him his large debts, and he then goes out and demands his small debt from a fellow slave. For this, he cannot be forgiven, because he has not learned the lesson from his Lord. He should be like him and do as he does.

God does not end with a full stop, but with a comma.

God always leaves the door open for acceptance and repentance. In fact, I rather prefer the word acceptance to the word forgiveness. It has a more positive slant and it expresses a lot more about the nature of the Christian Gospel. It was the American theologian Paul Tillich who made the comment 'Accepting acceptance is to have the courage to accept oneself as accepted in spite of being unacceptable.'[27]

God accepts us despite the fact that we know we are unacceptable. The door is kept open; the possibility of acceptance is always there. Many times God's acceptance is ignored or rejected. But that is no reason to stop being open and accepting even if it is done at a great cost to ourselves. We cannot afford to be too judgmental about others because we never know the exact nature of other people's circumstances or what pressures and strains they are under. Nor do we know enough about ourselves most of the time. But a loving, open acceptance of others is, in the long run, far more likely to bring good and positive results. Matthew leaves the possibility of a condemnation to hell, but that is not for us to do (even if we believe there is a hell). We need rather to treat others in the same way that God treats us - with a comma, not a full stop. I have lived for many years with a poem, which Dietrich Bonhoeffer wrote in his prison cell in 1944. It sums it all up. It is called CHRISTIANS AND PAGANS:[28]

Men go to God when they are sore bestead.
Pray to him for succour, for his peace, for bread,
For mercy for themselves, sinning or dead;
All men do so, Christians and unbelieving.

Men go to God when he is sore bestead,
Find him poor and scorned, without shelter or bread,
Whelmed under weight of the wicked, the weak, the
                    dead;
Christians stand by God in his hour of grieving.

God goes to every man when sore bestead,
Feeds body and spirit with his bread;
For Christians, pagans alike he hangs dead,
And both alike forgiving.

A comma, not a full stop.

27. p. 264, Tillich, P.(2000, 2nd. revised ed.) *The Courage to Be*, Yale: Yale University Press
28. Bonhoeffer, D. *Christians and Pagans*, p. 549 in Kelly & Nelson, 1990

On Leadership
Sermon given at Worcester Cathedral Advent II 1990

Hebrews 13: 7:
Remember your leaders who spoke God's message to you. Keep before you the outcome of their life and follow the example of their faith.

Last weekend the German people went to the polls to elect a new Chancellor for the whole of Germany. This was the first time that this has happened since 1932. A year later in January 1933 Adolf Hitler became Chancellor of Germany. At a time when many in Germany and indeed Britain welcomed the emergence of this strong leader, one voice stood out. This was the voice of Dietrich Bonhoeffer who, the day after Hitler's election, broadcast a talk entitled *The Leader (Führer) and the Individual in the Younger Generation*[29]. He pointed out that the massive cultural shift caused by the First World War had led to a vacuum in leadership especially for the young. It was from the youth movement that a new concept of leader had emerged. Let me give you two quotations from this talk:

> The Leader is set at a tremendous distance from those whom he leads, but - and this the decisive factor - he is Leader only as the one chosen by those whom he leads; as the one who has grown from among them, he received his authority only from his followers, from below from the people. The spirit of the people - so one imagines - summons the Leader from its metaphysical depths and raises him to the heights. This Leader, deriving from the concentrated will of the people, now appears as longingly awaited by the people, the one who is to fulfil their capabilities and potentialities. Thus the originally matter-of-fact idea of political authority has become the political, messianic concept of the Leader as we know it today. Into it there also streams all the religious thought of its adherents. Where the spirit of the people is a divine, metaphysical factor, the Leader who embodies this spirit has religious functions, and is in the proper sense the Messiah. With his appearance the fulfilment of the last hope has dawned.

So he analyses the situation in his diary. He sees danger in a leader claiming too much for himself.

The individual is responsible before God. And this solitude of man's position before God, this subjection to an ultimate authority, is destroyed

29. Reproduced in several volumes, e.g. Green & DeJonge (2013).

35

when the authority of the Leader or of the office is seen as ultimate authority. The irrefutable sign of man's individuality is that he must die alone, that he must bear his body for himself, that he must bear his suffering and his guilt as an individual. Alone before God, man becomes what he is, free and committed in responsibility at the same time. He becomes an individual. And this individual now knows himself to be in community. Community is only where man becomes an individual before God, and men; it is a community of suffering, of guilt, of death and of life. The fearful danger of the present time is that above the cry for authority, be it of the Leader or of an office, we forget that man stands alone before the ultimate authority and anyone who lays violent hands on man here is infringing eternal laws and taking upon himself superhuman authority which will eventually crush him. Thus the Leader points to the office, but Leader and office together point to the final authority itself, before which Reich or state are penultimate authorities. Leaders or offices which set themselves up as gods mock God and the individual who stands alone before him, and must perish.

The leader who claims ultimate authority – even when people treat him as a messiah – must inevitably perish, as indeed Hitler did, but not without terrible cost to vast numbers of humanity.

Recent weeks have forced us to look at questions of leadership and today is Bible Sunday so I thought it might be helpful to look at some other aspects of leadership and what the Bible can tell us about them. We may begin with Bonhoeffer's point that leadership is derived both from the people and from God. Both aspects have to be respected, otherwise leadership crumbles. If we look at a few Biblical characters, we can see various aspects emerging.

Abraham is the prime leader of Israel. His authority derives supremely from God as he is called out on an unknown journey to find a new land for his people. There must be a pioneering spirit in leadership which takes risks and goes off in new directions. We see some of this also in Moses but much more besides. Moses clearly stands in this middle position mediating the laws of God to the people and leading them out of slavery to the promised land. We see in Moses a leader who learns how to delegate and share authority with those around him, who realises that he cannot bear the burdens of leadership alone. He appoints judges to help him. Leadership becomes a shared partnership.

King David on the other hand revealed a leader, chosen by God, whose human frailty is there for all to see and by his attractive personality manages to help the people together and pass on real tasks to Solomon, his son.

It is of course in Jesus the Son of David that we see all this coming together. Jesus knowing his authority is derived from God speaks with authority and not at the scribes, at the same time he works in a corporate manner. He shares all but the ultimate with his disciples. He sends them out to proclaim the Kingdom. He entrusts them with the message. He is not always breathing down their necks. He invites them to share the ultimate within him but they fail to live up to the call.

Jesus shows supremely the nature of responsibility in leadership as he takes upon himself the effects of the evil and sins of humanity and suffers for his people on the cross. Here is true leadership. He knows where responsibility lies. His image of the leader is not a dominant person but a slave and a servant. He comes not to be ministered unto but to minister and to give up his life as a ransom for many. We see in Jesus one who encourages others to take responsibility. Not to take it away from them. Many of his answers to people are in fact questions which only the questioner can answer. Like the true therapist he does not solve problems for people but helps them to solve them for themselves.

Leadership thus pioneers, consults, enables, delegates, listens, but also by the telling of stories, by example - and by a willingness to take responsibility - builds up a community where all may care for each other. This was the vision which the early church discovered and summed up in the word *Koinonia*, fellowship, sharing and caring.

Remember your leaders, says the writer to the Hebrews, who spoke God's message to you. *Keep before you the outcome of their life and follow the example of their faith*. The writer to the Hebrews sees Jesus as the pioneer who goes before us and sees the saints and martyrs as those who follow in his way. He points to the martyrs as the example.

By their fruits ye shall know them, Jesus says. We can see those styles of leadership which dominate people, trample on them, refuse to listen and are sure they are right. We can see in Hitler what the fruit of that is. Self-destruction bus also destruction of many others.

All of us play leadership roles in one-way or another. We can look to Jesus, the author and finisher of our faith, to see what leadership really means. This is very vital at this time. For we too are witnessing a massive cultural shift throughout the world. There is a broad new openness, a new rediscovery of identity and new search for meaning. In such a situation the role of leadership is vital, for there is much fear about, there are those who would still seek dominance and power for their own ends and not responsible leadership for the good of the wider world. We all need to look to our leader Jesus and learn from him, for as Bonhoeffer also puts it:

> Should the leader allow himself to succumb to the wishes of those he leads, who always seek to turn him into their idol, the image of the leader will become the image of the misleader... This is the leader who makes an idol of himself and who thus mocks God.

Being Open
Sermon given at St. Georges, Sheffield
24th June 1973

Hebrews 13: v.13:
Let us therefore go forth to him outside the camp bearing abuse for him.

Trying to define a Christian is a very difficult thing. We may think we know what a Christian is - to others it may appear as something very different. We might like to think that a Christian is an open, loving, caring person. And yet James Baldwin can say of Christianity that with its rise came the denial of: 'a certain kind of spontaneity, a certain kind of joy, a certain kind of freedom, which a man can only have when he is in touch with himself, his surroundings, his women and his children.'[30]

We may think that Christians should love more than others and yet look at Northern Ireland, look at the Dutch Reformed Church in South Africa, look at ourselves. An interesting article in New Society the week before last asked the question 'Why are Christians prejudiced?' and reported on a survey of those groups which combine deep Christian convictions with high levels of prejudice. The conclusions of the survey were that those who were most prejudiced either expressed a nominal Christian commitment but practised it little, or were very narrow minded, deeply committed fundamentalist Christians who were reacting in fear against the uncertain, the unknown and the risky. So the writer argues:

'Religion partly comes from the fears of various kinds (such as God, death, hell) while ethnocentrism is partly based on other fears (such as people who are different and unpredictable). The overlap between these two characteristics is then attributed to their common ground - namely response to uncertainty.'[31] Let us therefore go forth to him outside the camp bearing abuse for him.

The passage from the Epistle to the Hebrews which was read earlier is one which commentators argue over frequently, and I do not wish to take you into the delicacies of this debate. I simply wish to point out that the writer is trying to get the 'Hebrews', whoever they were, to respond to a new situation, to move out from the safety of the Jewish

---

30. 'White Racism or World Community?' James Baldwin. Address to the 1968 Uppsala Assembly of the World Council of Churches. Reported in *The Ecumenical Review* Vol. 22 No. 4, October 1968, p.375
31. 'Why are Christians prejudiced?' Glenn Wilson. *New Society* 14th June 1973, p.618

Sacrificial system into something more risky and uncertain. Jesus goes outside the camp, bearing with him the reproaches, like the sin offering, which are the result of the sins and the fear of the community. Earlier the writer of the Epistle has compared Jesus to his namesake Joshua who was the pioneer who blazed the trail from the wilderness into the promised land. The Jesus who is always the same is always ahead of us - he goes before - he leads the way. He does not fear the unknown - he is willing to take risks, make experiments and not cling to the known. He goes outside the camp and he calls us to follow him.

I have taken much inspiration and hope from this theme for many years. It speaks to where I hope to stand - to what I wish to be as a person who is open to the world, to God and to others, and who is willing to take the risks which this involves. And I wish to be like this because this is the Christ I see in the Gospels. Jesus does not seem to me to call men[32] to conform to a pattern but to call them to be truly themselves and they can only do this when fear is cast aside and we step out from where we are to somewhere else.

For not all Christians are prejudiced - because not all are filled with fear. The article I quoted earlier end by remarking that there are some Christians who:

> are so fully assimilated into the religious environment that they can hardly avoid becoming committed to the ethical code of their religion, which usually includes an emphasis on "love of fellow men." Thus, sandwiched between the nominal church members and the fundamentalists, they remain a "truly Christian" group who express relatively little intolerance of other groups.[33]

and even James Baldwin hopes that the Church will rediscover its true shape:

> When a structure, a State or a Church or a country, becomes too expensive for the world to afford, when it is no longer responsive to the needs of the world, that structure is doomed. If the Christian faith does not recover its Lord and Saviour Jesus Christ, we shall discover the meaning of what he meant when he said, "Insofar as you have done it unto the least of these, you have done it unto me."[34]

---

32. Eds: again, we have retained the unfortunately gendered original prose throughout this chapter.
33. See footnote 31, p.619
34. See footnote 30, p.376

How then can we be open people? What does it mean to be an open Christian? I would list some attributes as follows:

1. He does not cling to false certainties.

Faith and certainty do not go together. The man who is certain in his faith has lost it. We need not fear any new knowledge or discovery; we simply need to see how it relates to our faith, not whether it threatens it. The fundamentalist is not only intellectually dishonest - for he claims to know what he cannot know - he is also encouraging an intolerance and establishing criteria which limit and restrict him as well as others. We too easily confuse ultimate things with the penultimate things, as Bonhoeffer put it. Only God is ultimate - the rest is relative to that and is not to be idolised whether it is the Church, the Bible, medical expertise, art, music - none are absolute and we should not claim that any of them are. If we believe in God, none of them possibly can be. Thus faith in God opens up new areas of life - to explore and to share with others.

2. The open Christian accepts others.

The basic Christian understanding is that God accepts and loves us just as we are. Because we know ourselves as accepted in spite of being unacceptable (to use Tillich's phrase). We are set free to accept others just as they are and not to try to force them into any particular mould. So much so-called evangelism is the attempt by some to force people to conform to some model of Christianity which they have themselves. Why do they do this? The answer must be because they are a minority which is not too clear about themselves, and wish to bolster each other up by pressurising others to be like them. True Christian evangelism is based on the reverse principle which says to people - be yourself - you don't have to pretend to be anything else. God knows and accepts what you are like anyhow. You can't impress God - so why try?

3. The open Christian accepts life as a whole:

He does not divide it into categories. There is not a religious bit, a work bit, a marriage or sex bit, a political bit. It is all one to be seen as one and experienced as one in which God is encountered in all experience, and all can be a means of love and service.

4. The open Christian is more concerned about the needs of others than his own needs.

Some people (and clergy among them) are so busy meeting

41

their own needs that they build little worlds around themselves and use others for their own ends. The open person is 'at ease in the world' and is therefore sensitive to the cries for help around him. Of course he cannot bear them alone, nor should he, but he may very well meet his own deepest needs by being more concerned for others. So he will also tend to listen more than to speak - for listening is a way of caring and helping which only one who is open to others can use.

5. The open Christian will not fear change.

This does not mean that all change is necessarily good. It may have to be protested against - even rejected or rebelled against if it dehumanises men, but change itself is not to be feared, again rather to be used creatively.

6. The open Christian will be a relaxed person.

In a recent article on dying the Revd. Geoffrey Harding points out that sleep is a sort of dying and should be seen as a dying to self. Each day we should die to that day. He writes: 'It is not enough to commit ourselves to the care of God; obviously we must uncommit ourselves to everything else, in order to be really "open" to tomorrow.'[35]

If this commitment and assurance that God will lead us, that Christ goes before us outside the camp, is ours - then we can relax - we can let things happen - we do not have to justify ourselves. 'If we believe (we are open),' he concludes, 'we have life eternal (already)'. An openness to God through relaxed and relaxing prayer may well be the key way in which we may die to ourselves and be set free to be open to people in the world.

Ephphatha - BE OPENED said Jesus to the one who was deaf and dumb. It is a word to us all and if our faith is to be loving rather than prejudiced, if our faith is to be creative rather than destructive - if we are in fact to have faith at all - we all need to be opened more and more to the world, to others and to God in Christ Jesus who is our pioneer - who goes before us and who therefore calls us to go with him outside the camp, away from the securities we cling to - to the uncertainties, the suffering, the joy which we see in Jesus Christ.

---

35. Death and Dying". G. Harding. *New Fire* No. 15, Summer 1973, p.289

One Dean's Pipe Dreams
An article for the Friends of Cathedral Music
April 1989

Cathedrals are in the news. Handling the media is now becoming a required skill for Deans and Provosts. It is an opportunity to share the faith and to explain the problems cathedrals face. But it could also be a snare and a trap. People will only be interested either if there is a news story, or if there is a real vision to share.

'*Guard the Vision entrusted to you*'. Those words are used to someone being admitted into the Little Gidding Community. They could well be words for those working in cathedrals. But if we are to guard the vision we must first seek to understand the vision of those who first built our cathedrals. They, on the whole, had two main visions. One was to create a building for community, the other was to seek to worship and express the glory of God. These are right and proper motives still and ones we can share.

But cathedrals are not places to romanticise about. They are places where all the normal ups and downs of human life are seen and experienced. If we are to have visions they must be visions firmly placed in reality. Nothing happens by magic, all is hard work. People get upset, people need help, relationships have to be nurtured just as they do in any family or place of work. The first requirement of any real vision is that it is fixed firmly in the real world. Otherwise it will lead to frustration and anger as false and unreal expectations are not met. Community consists of being able to cope with the ups and downs of human relationships. Some of the wisest words about community are found in Bonhoeffer's book *Life Together* (1954).

So we first get it clear that a cathedral is a very earthly place full of the usual earthly problems of life. But we do not stop there. We seek a vision both of what a cathedral has been and also of what a cathedral can be. Thus we see the second part of preparing for a vision. That is understanding our roots, seeing how we got to where we are.

In a cathedral environment this is a daunting task. The scale of everything is so large, the history so immense. But we must try; realising that what we grasp will only be partial and always subject to amendment as more knowledge comes to light. When I came to Worcester I read the previous forty years' Chapter Minutes. That was one way of coming to terms with earthly realities and seeing what the roots were!

The former Provost of Southwark Ernie Southcott had a great

adage: 'You can't take people from where they are not to somewhere they don't want to be'. A real vision must begin from where we now are. If it is to be a corporate vision the community will also have to share the same perception. This is very difficult to achieve. Good communication takes a long time.

Cathedrals have never been visited more than they are now. They could easily slip into being commercial tourist centres, but they can be much more than that. Cathedrals can be places of dreams and visions which open us all up to become new and different people. What then are the ingredients?

SPACE. We all need space to be creative. Cathedrals show us how space can be used to express the skill of people and the grandeur of God. People do not need to be harassed or impressed when they visit a cathedral. They need rather space to stand and reflect. Cathedrals would all look much better without any seating in them. It would force the individual into a reflection of space and size and of their own insignificance. In a still space we may learn to meditate and pray.

COLOUR. Some people are supposed to dream in colour, others in black and white. Cathedrals should emanate colour, in windows, in decoration, in frontals and vestments, in needlework and carpet. On the whole we are not bold enough. There are few places which match Coventry Cathedral for impact of colour both in windows and tapestry. It communicates both grandeur and complexity; it prevents us from seeing a single faceted God. The glory of God is many coloured. Gerald Manley Hopkins expressed this in his poem 'Glory be to God for dappled things'.

SOUND. The sound of cathedrals is perhaps too limited. Some musicians will be more experimental than others in the use of music. The rich tapestry of music is all needed and to be held with the power of the architecture. Is it essential the music simply be that of cathedral choirs, organs and the occasional orchestra? What about the use of new electronic sound? What about attracting buskers, like those we hear on the London Underground, to perform in corners of cathedrals? A guitarist in the Lady Chapel, a saxophonist in the Crypt? What about the sound of dramatic speech or poetry reading? Sound too can have a deep impact in our mind. Presentations in sound, colour and picture may well be possible to draw attention to the mystery of God.

SYMBOL. Much truth is communicated through symbolism. At some times of the year, notably Christmas and Easter we see a lot of symbolism in worship but what about the rest of the year? Do not many Gospel stories open themselves to other symbols? The water out of Caana, the baskets of loaves and fishes, the salt, the leaven, the light, fish in a net, seeds in the ground. Much more symbolism could come into our worship each week. When we draw up our liturgy we should ask more fully what choreography, symbolism and movement might be included.

MOVEMENT. Dame Ninette de Valois always wanted the ballet Job performed in St. Paul's Cathedral. We still do not have enough use made of dance in worship though we are getting better at it. Perhaps in some ways there is too much movement in cathedrals, people are too active. Maybe we need to help people to learn to move quietly and reverently. The way we move can be a form of prayer.

CREATIVITY. Schools, colleges, even libraries often have artists in residence or writers in residence - why not cathedrals? Where people would see an artist at work, a sculptor making a new shape, a musician composing, a poet reading his new poems. Others would be stirred to find new gifts within themselves as a result.

SHARING. Cathedrals should be places of sharing. Sharing food, sharing ideas, offering help to those in need. I have a vision of the Crypt at Worcester providing counselling, support and healing for those in need. The sharing of life is implicit in the Gospel. In what we do we should ask the question How can we share this?

'Guard your Vision'. But everyone's vision will be different. What we need to do is to create the conditions for people to find their own vision by opening up new ways for ourselves and others. Cathedrals should take us out of ourselves and into ourselves. Out of ourselves, to aspire to new possibilities. Into ourselves, to discover new depths and deeper understanding of our own identity. Here we begin to turn full circle, for these conditions will not become a reality unless the cathedral community shares a vision and has the sort of life which will create these conditions. It will only be real if the harsh realities of daily living, financial viability and good management and organisation are all in place. So the Dean may have his dreams but he must also work at them with others. If not his dreams will become nightmares. What is clear is that we have been in danger of being too turned in on ourselves when in fact cathedrals are one of the Church's greatest assets for mission and one of the most exciting laboratories for Christian experimentation. So we must guard our vision by our prayer, by our encounter and sharing with others and by ensuring that we see the hand of God in every mundane aspect of life, as well as in the most sublime.

(Originally published in:
The Friends of Cathedral Music: 32nd Annual Report, April 1989)

It Could Be You!

Sermon given for the Civic Service,
Worcester Cathedral, 11 June 1995

Ecclesiastes 3: v.18:
In dealing with human beings it is God's purpose to test them and to see what they truly are.

"It Could Be You!" says the Lottery advert. It could be you, but know it won't be. You should be grateful for that fact. Do you recall Studdert Kennedy's poem *If I had a Million Pounds?*[36]

I would build me a perfect island
Sweet set in a southern sea
   And then would I build me Paradise
For the heart o' my Love and me.

I would plant me a perfect garden there
The one that my dream soul knows,
   And the year would flow as the petals grow,
That flame to a perfect rose.

I would build me a perfect temple there,
   A shrine where my Christ might dwell,
And then I would wake to behold my soul
   Damned deep in a perfect Hell.

The National Lottery (a form of Income Tax for the gullible, which has lost charities £71 million in four months) is just a sign that we are moving towards fantasyland. We do not or cannot face the real world, so we choose, and we are encouraged to live in, a fantasy world; a world where we win the lottery; a world where we can get lots of money without working for it; a world which cuts us off from other people and enables us to forget and ignore their plight. The psychologists tell us that fantasy is indulged in by individuals who are isolated and devalued, who fail in real activity and so, like Walter Mitty, find satisfaction imagining life in an unreal world. The Lottery is not the cause of this. It is just a symptom of a sick society. There are many others. The recent AGM of British Gas revealed the total failure of the Directors to understand why people were angry with them.

---

36 Studdert Kennedy, G.A. (1927) *The Unutterable Beauty*, p.113

Examining the role of the intellectual in wartime Britain, and comparing it with today, Richard Weight, a student of British identity, has summed up our present situation in these words:

> After the 1960s, Britain continued its inexorable decline from a nation of shopkeepers into a nation of tourist guides...The conservation movement ballooned in the 1970s spawning such organisations as the Campaign for Real Ale. And in more recent years, what has become known as the 'heritage industry' has even turned the remnants of Britain's industrial infrastructure into museums and theme parks. Today many critics once again scoff at the parochial class ridden nature of Britain and its obsession with the glories of the past as a way of masking the failures of the present.[37]

So we prefer a life of fantasy. We prefer to live in a theme park, rather than face the realities, because the realities are very unpleasant.

For this is a society where, since 1979, the rich have got 63 per cent richer while the poor have got 17 per cent poorer.[38] A country where one in three children grows up in poverty, one in five men of working age is not working, one seven 21-year olds have trouble reading and more than one million pensioners live on income support.[39]

A country where the drug trade is leading to a massive increase in crime (and drugs themselves are part of a fantasy world). A country which seeks to keep itself going economically by engaging in dubious massive arms trading, and living off the fruits of third world debt, which has recently been described as 'the modern form of slavery'. A nation where the pollution of the environment is positively encouraged by our lifestyle and where many standards of public and private morality seem to be ignored if they do not suit our personal convenience. We are all caught up in it, whether we like it or not. So when many people find themselves undervalued and ignored, fantasy is all that is left.

What has gone wrong is that we are becoming part of a dysfunctional society. This is not fundamentally a political or social problem but a human and religious one. People are increasingly disillusioned by the processes of the political machine, which seems concerned with self-preservation and ideology rather than people's real

---

37. Weight, Richard, 'Return to Albion: Intellectuals in Wartime Britain', *History Today*, Vol. 44 (12) December 1994
38. Recent Rowntree Trust survey (source unknown, Eds.)
39. Quoted in 'Social Justice - the way ahead', Borrie, Sir Gordon, *Royal Society of Arts Journal*, Vol. CXLIII No. 5457, March 1995

needs. We see this in education, the health services and other areas. I see exactly the same taking place inside the Church, where the institution, instead of serving people, is simply seeking to preserve itself. So people are going off into fantasy religion and isolationist practices.[40] In Church and society there is a dysfunction between the role of the institution, serving its own needs, and the real needs of people, which are becoming ignored. We have lost our way. People are becoming lost and isolated. We can only live with isolation by building up a world of fantasy be it gambling, pornography, fantasy films or the world of virtual reality. We refuse to face the reality about ourselves. We fail to see who we really are.

The writer of Ecclesiastes gives us a clue. Not only must we do things at the right time and keep in tune with the rhythm of the world and of other people, we must also seek to see things as they truly are. For that is what God does.

We have to acknowledge the fantasies and reject them. Failure to do so will lead to even more serious neurosis. We have to look at the dysfunction between institutional life and people. This we can only do by rejecting the prevalent mood of individualism and realise that we are a social people. That we are an interdependent people, who cannot live without each other.

We are living in an age of such massive scientific and technical change that we are unable to assimilate properly our own inventions. The Oxford philosopher, John Gray, commenting on the development of the Internet and the superhighway has written:

The danger of the new technology is that allied with a techno-Utopian ideology, they will be used to distract us from increasing poverty and isolation in our everyday lives. Virtual communities are surrogates for the communities we are fast losing. In schools and neighbourhoods, in streets and workplaces, human exchanges have an unfathomable depth of meaning that no computer can simulate. The mirage of virtual community serves to reconcile us to the growing dereliction of the social institutions and public places in which these unprogrammed encounters occur. If cities are desolated and schools stalked by fear, if we shrink from strangers and children as threats to our safety, a retreat into the empty freedom of cyberspace may seem like liberation. Yet living much of our lives in this space means giving up part of what makes us human.[41]

40. cf. the debate over the 'Toronto Blessing' especially the writings of Rd. Martyn Percy, Chaplain of Christ's College, Cambridge, and the BBC 'Everyman' programme of 21 May, 1995
41. Gray, J. "The Sad Side of Cyberspace", *Guardian*, 1995

Community, which enables people to be valued and respected, is being destroyed.

This is Trinity Sunday, when we reflect on the fact that God in whose image we are made is a community of Father Son and Holy Spirit. The first thing God our creator will expect of us is to come to terms with our own frail humanity and the humanity of others and admit who we really are.

'The life of God', says Bishop Rowan Williams, 'constantly works against the state of mutual isolation in which human beings live'.[42] He goes on to argue the whole point of the Christian message is to enable us to reach out beyond ourselves; discovering that, because God loves and accepts us, we can reach out to others. As God in Christ has held nothing back so we cannot hold back from total self-giving. We can be saved from fantasyland only when we realise that 'It could be You'.

It could be you whom God loves and accepts just as you are.
It could be you who is thereby set free to reach out to those in isolation and consequent fantasy.
It could be you who with your neighbours seeks community instead of competition, giving instead of getting, serving others instead of serving ourselves.

But it will only be you if you are willing to take the risk which God in Christ takes, of letting go of everything and working this out in the pain and agony of the real world, instead of in the unreal world of fantasy and virtual reality.

The whole point of faith in God is that it gives proper perspective. It stops us becoming God ourselves, it prevents making ourselves the centre of life. It means that the first thing we have to do is affirm our humanity and to assert the humanity of each other. This leads us to denounce all that destroys humanity.

Our world needs communities of protest to denounce all that denies human potential. The future of the Church lies in being a community of protest rather than a society of religious self-preservation.

So there is a task here for every one of us. In our homes, in our street, in our locality as well as in the wider world. To cast out the fantasy and face the reality. To look beyond ourselves and rebuild community. To find a new vision for community and to avoid a perfect hell. For if our world really did have a purpose, people would not want to live on

---

42. Williams, R. 'Doing the Works of God'in *Open to Judgement*, 1994

drugs; if we did have vision we would not need pornography; if we were building community, we would not want to wish to trade in arms and world debt.

It could be you - taking responsibility not just for yourself, but for others. It could be you, affirming life and building community. For unless you and I start now, we shall escape further into fantasy and we shall continue to destroy ourselves and others.

Christian Concerns for the Future

Conservative Party Conference

6th October 1993

It was kind of you to invite me. Since accepting your invitation, I have been reading a lot of background material, for I am not a politician and not a political thinker. An unusual book was Julian Critchley's *Floating Voter* which describes a murder at the Conservative Party Conference in Brighton last year. You will know better than me whether it is accurate or not!

I am not a member of any political party but as one who tries to inform his political views from his Christian understanding, I want to show you how my mind works. You may think it is very confused!

My theme today is 'Christian Concerns for the Future.' What I wish to do is to make some preliminary comments about the Christian understanding of people and society (based on two biblical passages) and then to pin-point what seems to me to be the matters of priority of the future of our world.

My first text is from St Matthew's Gospel 22 v 15-2. It is a familiar passage.

Then the Pharisees went away and agreed on a plan to trap him in argument. They sent some of their followers to him together with members of Herod's party. "Teacher," they said, "we know you are a sincere man; you teach in all sincerity the way of life that God requires, courting no man's favour, whoever he may be. Give us your ruling on this are we or are we not permitted to pay taxes to the Roman Emperor?" Jesus was aware of their malicious intention and said, "You hypocrites! Why are you trying to catch me out? Show me the coin used for the tax." They handed him a silver piece. Jesus asked, "Whose image is in this superscription?" "Caesar's," they replied. He said to them, "Then pay to Caesar what belongs to Caesar and to God what belongs to God."

This passage at first glance points to a debate between church and state, but at a deeper level opens up a debate about the nature of humanity. In this passage the Pharisees seem to be playing politics. How are people to act in an occupied territory? Jesus will not engage in the fruitless game of playing off the Church against the state. The image on the coin is that of Caesar, so it belongs to Caesar. Man is made in the image of God, so man owes everything to God and finds his significance in God. The obligations of citizenship are part of our discipleship. To

51

say that everything belongs to God radically changes the way we look at the world. As Christians believe that the nature of God is most fully revealed in Jesus, so that the nature of humanity is best expressed in the person of Jesus. This means that the closer we become to Jesus, the closer we come to our real nature. That is the fundamental motive for the imitation of Christ and for our Christian discipleship.

What do we, who are made in God's image, discover? We learn that the basic message of life is loving and self-giving. We learn that, like Jesus, we may have to stand against current trends and ideas. Christians are called to be centres of protest against all that dehumanises and diminishes people. We learn that the price of love is suffering. We learn that triumphant living comes from the surrender of our identity, not clinging to it. We discover that the essence of responsibility is not responsibility for myself, but responsibility for my neighbour, for the down trodden, for the outcast and for the poor.

We also see that essential nature of man is not individual but corporate. Christians believe that God is expressed as Trinity in unity: in that total self-giving of the persons of the Holy Trinity to each other. God, in whose image we are made, is community. Under God, we are all interdependent in our very nature. What we are and do affects other people. Churchmen are always being called to give a moral lead and it is here I believe that we can discover the basis for morality. Scripture is full of corporate understanding of humankind summed up in that strange phrase in the Epistle to the Hebrews 'They without us shall not be made perfect' (10 v. 40). True humanity is shared, corporate and willing to give to the uttermost.

We all belong to each other and are responsible for each other. I like Malcolm Boyd's adage 'My brother does not want a keeper - he wants a brother.'[43] Let us look at some implications of this:

1. We hear a great deal about extending people's freedom of choice, but if I belong to my brother and he belongs to me then I cannot exercise and do not have a freedom of choice which is not his as well. I do not believe, for example, that I can morally opt for private education or private medicine unless that is a real choice for everyone and while it is only an option for 10% of the population, I have no moral right to follow that path. I agonise over this matter because I know that I am not wholly consistent but I do believe that there is a deep moral principle here. Do I really have a freedom of choice if it is a choice which is not available to others?

43. Boyd, M. (1968) *Malcolm Boyd's Book of Days*, London: SCM Press

2. I am frequently told that people have the right to do what they like with their money. I do not believe it. If I belong to God, then nothing I have belongs to me. It belongs to God and I can only use it in ways which are consistent to the will of God. If people spend their money to encourage drug addiction, to promote pornography, to encourage the sale of armaments these are not choices that are really free to make because they cannot be consistent with the will of God. There is a contractual aspect to the use of money as well. Ever since I was a curate in a very poor area of Sunderland in the late 1950s, I have been unable to justify gambling as in any way desirable. Gambling is above all a contractual affair. I cannot gamble unless other people do. When you see the poverty wrought through compulsive gambling, you have to realise that if you did not gamble other people would not be able to. If there is even one person whose life is ruined through gambling, I have no moral right to gamble. We do no good by developing a culture in which the desire for gain and greed is deliberately encouraged.

3. What I am really getting at here is that morality has a contractual basis. Because we belong to each other, our behaviour affects everyone else. If we wish to have a moral society, we have to move away from the extreme emphasis of self-fulfilment, personal satisfaction and move to encouraging a sense of mutual responsibility and sharing.

This corporate understanding of humanity lies deep in the Christian ethic. Morality covers every aspect of life - not just the individual one. What for instance is the morality of building up an economy by encouraging the arms trade? We are increasingly concerned about the way cigarettes kill people but unwilling to give up the banning of advertising and the tax benefits. The promotion of an economy based on the sale of weapons to kill seems to me to be even more immoral. If there was no arms trade, many of today's wars could not happen. The fact that other people might sell arms is no reason for us to do so. The arms for Iraq investigations reveals what a very murky business this is.

My second biblical passage is in St Luke Gospel (4: v. 16ff) where Jesus goes into the synagogue and reads the passage from Isaiah. *'The spirit of the Lord is upon me because he has anointed me. He has sent me to preach goods news to the poor; to proclaim liberty to the captives, the recovery of sight to the blind, to let the broken victims go free. To proclaim the year of the Lord's Favour.'* Jesus is the Christ, the anointed one, he comes to preach from the Kingdom where God rules. So he announces the Jubilee.

Just as the seventh day was the day of rest, so the seventh year was the day when slaves were released. Ezekiel pleaded that every seventh year the slaves should be freed but he complains that the command is not being kept. But that was not the Jubilee. The Jubilee was the fiftieth year. Seven times seven years. This was a year for freedom for all. It was announced with the sound of a trumpet. The fields were all to remain fallow; every man entered into his ancestral property. Lands purchased were returned (you bought a number of harvests, not the land). Debtors and slaves were set free. It was a time of restitution; a time to start afresh. For everything belonged to God. Nothing could be sold absolutely. The Jubilee was of profound social and political significance. It was a way of controlling man's power and greed. It was a way of achieving equality. But, (and it is a big BUT), Old Testament scholars tell us the Jubilee was never kept. It appeared too impractical. Man's greed got the better of him. So Roland de Vaux writes, 'It was a utopian law and it remained a dead letter.'[44]

We know that the world into which Jesus was born was a very unjust one. So Duncan Derrett, commenting on the social exploitation of Jesus' day, writes:

> The activities of thieves and robbers show that the receivers of stolen property and secret sympathisers with brigands must have existed. The temple hierarchy and successful capitalists showed, by their accumulations and conspicuous consumption, that the economy, based on strict application of the law of real property was not operating in the spirit of brotherhood of all Israel. The threat of the Jubilee…did nothing to prevent the accumulation of lands in relatively few hands…No attempt was made to deal with the root cause of financial inequality. [45]

It was into this situation that Jesus came proclaiming that the Jubilee had come. He proclaimed what many longed for. Yet it was already part of the law. Not only did He proclaim it, but by his crucifixion and resurrection He achieved it. It is as if Jesus was saying 'Live out the law of God, otherwise the Jubilee will never come.' So the rich young man is asked to keep the law, sell all he has, and give to the poor. 'Jubilee is possible,' Jesus seems to be saying, 'if you believe it and live by it.' That is why Jesus is concerned about the rich. They have the power to enable the Jubilee to become a reality. They can, by

44. De Vaux, R. (1965) *Ancient Israel: Social Institutions*, New York: McGraw-Hill
45. Derrett, J. D. M. (1973), *Jesus's Audience: The Social and Psychological Environment in Which He Worked: Prolegomena to a Restatement of the Teaching of Jesus, Lectures at Newquay*, pp 77-78

redistributing wealth, assert the true community of humanity. The poor already share that community in their poverty. This is no spiritualised Gospel. This is the way of Christ.

Now if these are proper Christian insights what then are the concerns which Christians should have for the future? What will help bring in the Jubilee?

1. **Need for economic democracy**: Many Christian thinkers see this as a major Christian concern. There is a need for a just participatory and sustainable society. No one is seriously questioning the need for some sort of market economy but many are questioning whether it is enough in itself. A market economy is just as much open to manipulation as any other form of socialist or dictatorial economy. Indeed, in an age of extreme manipulation through advertising and the media, the power to create artificial and unnecessary markets is very frightening. The danger is that it reduces people to those who can be exploited to generate income. Our motto needs to be 'I am my brother's keeper, not my brother's competitor'. The market on its own is an impersonal power. We need an economy that seeks a common good and rejoices in the wealth which is people, rather than the cheque book. The other very great risk is that economic policy is dominated by the powerful forces of marketing and monopolies regardless as to whether what they are selling is good or bad in itself.

There is an urgent need to make a distinction between people's needs and people's wants. People have basic needs which have to be met to be human. What we want is another matter. In this context I cannot see the virtue of always reducing taxes. For income tax is one way of bringing in the Jubilee, of redistributing wealth in a just and equitable way. Of course governments should watch expenditure carefully and not tax people unnecessarily, but in terms of what meets people's basic needs (food, water, health, clothing, housing and education) surely taxation is the proper way of financing it. Income tax is the only method which will really work and justice requires that it is income which is taxed, not goods, otherwise the poor suffer again. The taxation system may need to be simplified. Maybe people should have more say about what the tax is used for by some form of referendum.

Similarly, we will not have a just society until we have thought much more carefully about the level in society at which things should be done. We have heard much about subsidiarity in recent years. Things should operate at the lowest possible level. This can and will work when people feel that they are empowered and trusted to get on with creating and sharing in the common good. People are motivated when they are trusted. This has been the secret of effective Christian mission and should be the basis of an economic democracy. We need many more intermediate structures where people can share and participate. As one writer has put it:

> Centralised government is an obvious recipe for incompetence even more than for tyranny. We need to restore a whole range of intermediate institutions...unions, professional organisations, local democratic government and voluntary and charitable bodies, not to mention the churches. Such bodies need to break up centralised power, to encourage participation, and restore morale to ordinary people by convincing them that they do count, that they are listened to, and they can participate.[46]

2. Peace: My second priority would be the search for a lasting peace. It may not be fully achievable but it must always be a priority. The dramatic and too fast changes in Eastern Europe have not brought peace, rather they have revealed new (possibly old) divisions. Ours is a deeply disturbed world. It is also a very unjust world. Most people (who in Christ are our brothers and sisters) live in terrible poverty. Very few are rich, and millions starve. Earlier this year I visited South Africa and visited the townships and squatter camps where millions live in squalor. It is profoundly unjust but it is really only a picture of the whole world. We are in relation to the rest of the world like the dominating whites in South Africa. While such injustice exists, we cannot live in peace or even be at peace in our minds. The unfairness of the Third World debt, the economic exploitation of many nations still has to be done away with. It will not be easy or simple, but I suspect it is of greater importance than getting our own economy right. Our self-concern to put our own house in order may be why we do not succeed. If we really did help Eastern Europe and the Third World a lot more we might find our own economy improved.

3. Racism: We need to tackle the deep pain of racism. Racism is an expression of fear, fear of those who are not like us. Racial violence emerges from racial suppression. Excessive dependence leads to violence and rejection. But as we look around the world we see racism rife, with ethnic cleansing, with racial conflict in European cities, with

---

46. Source unknown.

56

anti-Semitism and the refusal to understand Judaism or Islam. We see deep hatred which is profoundly destructive. Christians, Jews, Hindus, Buddhists and Muslims believe that we must love one another, including the stranger within our gates. The whole exercise of mutual understanding and dialogue between the religions is a vital part of preserving humanity at this time. Dialogue must be at the top of the Church's agenda. We all share our common humanity but equally we all have gifts to give to each other. A multi- racial, multi-cultural society is a richness to celebrate, not a loss of identity to bemoan.

4. Environment: We have to be concerned with the preservation of the environment. A market economy cannot solve the problems of the greenhouse effect but it has done a lot to create it. We cannot carry on relying on a car economy, which is doing so much to destroy the environment. Building roads simply generates more cars. If all the money being spent on roads was being channelled into accessible and affordable public transport, we could drastically reduce our dependence on the car with its accompanying problems. We do not need to be at the mercy of car manufacturers or road builders. If we have a real market economy, it will shift to meet the new needs. The great secrecy surrounding the environmental effects of nuclear power is profoundly disturbing. Are we putting the financial gain of some above the future of our planet? Nothing could be more immoral than that.

The Bible calls us the stewards of God's creation. We have to act responsibly with the world not exploit and destroy it. Time is running out, we cannot hand on to future generations a polluted and polluting world. Not only are we corporate beings, we are also interdependent with nature. In destroying the world, we are destroying ourselves. We are destroying the Image of God within us.

Economic democracy, world peace, removal of racism and the preservation of the environment, these are priorities.

Now this may seem very simplistic. For these are all highly complex issues, but this leads me to the last thing I want to say. We cannot resolve our problems to serve God's purposes by following any narrow ideology. Any dominant ideology be it communism, liberalism or conservatism leads to a simplistic and limited vision. As Thomas Cullinan has put it, "Reductions to simplicities become very plausible but in the process we limit the criteria for judging reality." Thus we reduce the perceived truth. Such ideologies have the effect of dividing society into those we accept the ideology and those who do not. Propaganda and marketing are ideal tools of ideologies because they also express ideas in a simplistic way. All this has the effect of making those who accept the ideology extremely self-righteous and makes those who do not accept it feel guilty, deprived, angry and frustrated. Thus people are either loyal or the enemy. Such techniques are no way to run any society, for they lack true respect for people. Any simplistic ideology does not match with a pluralistic and pluriform world. There are no simplistic answers. All we, as Christians can do, is try to be obedient to the image of Christ and seek to bring in his Jubilee.

Ours is a sad, dreary and sick society. Many of the things we moan about, increasing crime, breakdown of the family, the growth of the drugs trade and AIDS are simply the symptoms of a sick body and a sick society. They are the symptoms, not the cause. The causes lie in the failure to admit our corporate nature, our interdependence on nature and need to bring in the Jubilee. A stronger morality depends on a corporate and contractual view of the society, and one which rejects a doctrine of individualism.

In this context, the Christian Church cannot play the simple role of consecrating the status quo, which is what Caesar would always want; nor can it turn away into a pietistic corner, which is what dictators prefer. The Church, just because it has now been marginalised in society, can act as a broker of ideas, a service agency to bring differing views together at many levels. It can be a body which, because it seeks to follow Jesus and serve God, brings a new perspective into things. I hope that in the years to come, we can find a partnership not with any one political party, but with all and with many other groups to bring about a better world where people can be more truly themselves and God thus glorified.

Kafka in Blackpool
October 1993

A year ago I received an invitation from the Conservative Central Office to speak at the Conservative Christian Forum, a lunchtime fringe meeting at their Blackpool conference this year. I accepted the invitation and took it very seriously, talked to a lot of people, read a lot of books, and my final text went through nine drafts.

I never heard another word from Central Office, but Harry Greenway MP kept in touch and asked me to meet him on 6th October, the day of the talk at 12.45 at the Imperial Hotel, Blackpool. About ten days before, I realised that in order to be sure of being on time, I would have to come up the night before. I asked Mr. Greenway if accommodation could be provided. He consulted the Central Office and they said 'no, there was no room'. (On arrival in Blackpool I saw large numbers of hotels advertising vacancies). He did, however check with them that all the arrangements had been made for me and they confirmed they had.

I therefore arranged to stay with the Bishop of Blackburn as we were both at a meeting together in London the day before. He very kindly arranged transport to Blackpool for me. I reached the Imperial Hotel just after 10 a.m. to find it surrounded by the police. I told one policeman why I was there. He told me that as I had no pass, I had to go to a local Conservative Office which was dealing with accreditation to get one. I naturally assumed that they would have one ready for me. I walked about two miles to find the place and failed to do so. I decided it would be better if I went to the Winter Gardens to find Mr. Greenway. When I arrived there, I asked if someone could get Mr. Greenway out of the Conference to see me. I was told no. I had to go and get a valid pass. This time I was given the proper address and I took a taxi.

At the accreditation office, I was thoroughly searched and then allowed to go up to the room where the passes were issued. I asked for my pass and was told there wasn't one. 'Could they please get hold of Mr. Greenway?', I asked. They rang the Winter Gardens and left a message for him. There was nothing they could do for me. Would I go and get some photos taken for a pass? I refused; after all, the Central Office had invited me. It was their problem, not mine. By now it was 11.30 a.m. The talk was scheduled for 1 p.m. They relented a little and let me fill in a form. At 12.50, Mr. Greenway rang and got cut off. During all this time I was met with officiousness and not even offered a cup of tea.

At 1.10 p.m. Mr. Greenway arrived. They could do nothing without his signature. They found a Polaroid camera and took my picture.

At 1.20 we left. We arrived at the Winter Gardens at 1.35. I had a pass at last! I could get in. There was just enough time to at least deliver a summary of the talk. I had with me a briefcase with my talk and a small bag with overnight things in. 'You can't take that bag in here,' said the man on the door. A Chief Steward was called. We asked if there was somewhere the bag could be left. There was nowhere. Rules were rules and had to be kept, even though Central Office had not bothered to tell me anything about the Conference at all.

That was it. I exploded. "No wonder the Tory Party is in a Bloody Mess!" We went and had some lunch, and I returned to Worcester. Which thing is a parable.

Cold War

Worcester Cathedral

13th December 1987: Advent III

Matthew 11: v.22:
Ever since the coming of John the Baptist the Kingdom of Heaven has been subjected to violence and violent men are seizing it.

This week we have witnessed a significant breakthrough in the Cold War and in the pile up of nuclear weapons. I hope it does mean more peace, but there is still a long way to go and if some reports are to be believed much more sharing and understanding are needed. Thank God that process is under way.

For people live with visions, people are motivated by their own understanding of the way the world works and what makes it tick, and very often the terrible things which happen are the result of false visions, or rather delusions not really related to reality. The Marxist ideology has something of that about it - the vision of a world of total justice for the working classes - but the means to bring it about - the violence - the oppression - the fear - must make us question the vision itself.

We need not be one sided about this. What about the American Dream? The American vision which spills over into the Western world. In a new book[47] the rather eccentric writer Gore Vidal puts forward a very disturbing view of what has been making the American government tick. This vision behind Reagan's presidency he says is that he is to prepare us for the coming war between the Christ and the Anti-Christ - a war between the United States and Russia to take place in Israel.

According to Gore Vidal, in 1970 a group of fundamentalist American evangelists met with Reagan when he was Governor of California. They prayed with him and prophesied that he would be elected President. The following year Reagan lunched with Billy Graham and he asked Graham the following question: 'Do you believe that Jesus Christ is coming soon and what are the signs of his coming?' To which Billy Graham replied: 'The indication is that Jesus Christ is at the very door.'

Reagan apparently became obsessed with the book of the prophet Ezekiel and he is reported as having said: 'All of the other prophecies that had to be fulfilled before Armageddon have come to pass. In the thirty-eighth chapter of Ezekiel it says God will take the children of Israel from among the heathen and will gather them again into the promised land.

---

47. Eds: precise source unknown, but we think it is probably Vidal, G. (1987) *Armageddon? Essays 1983 – 1987*

For the first time ever everything is in place for the battle of Armageddon and the Second Coming of Christ.'

Now this attitude has been fermented in him by the Fundamentalist preachers and the writings of a man called Hal Lindsey. Not only was the end of the world in view, but much could be done to speed up the process. In their view there was no point in bothering about conservation - the Lord was coming. They considered the world to be an evil place which deserves to be destroyed. As a result of their preaching, 39% of Americans currently believe that the world will end in nuclear fire. The Lord and the American will win the battle of Armageddon, thanks to the Star Wars programme. The Anti-Christ Russia will perish and the Jews with them.

Thus in 1980 Reagan is reported as having said to (the now discredited) James Baker: 'We may be the generation that sees Armageddon.' But as Gore Vidal points out, when the encounters between Reagan and Gorbachev began Gorbachev turned out not to be the evil man Reagan expected. As Vidal puts it: 'The Lord of the Flies had not read the Good Book. If he had he would know that this planet is just a staging area for that glorious place in the sky where, free of abortion and contraception and communism, the chosen will swirl about in the cosmic dust praising the Lord for all eternity.'

The delusions become replaced when people meet face to face and their projections of each other fade away, reality breaks in. This is what seems to have been happening this week.

Now Vidal is no lover of the Christian religion but, faced with this sort of agenda, who would be? All Christians need to remember the cry: *O Assyria, Rod of my anger.*[48] God may well use the irreligious and the secular to save the religious from their delusions. Our Advent God is always unexpected.

'Since the coming of John the Baptist the Kingdom of Heaven has always been subjected to violence and violent men are seizing it.' These strange words of Jesus have been the subject of much critical consideration but the implication is fairly clear. It is God who brings in the Kingdom in his own way, in his own time. It is the arrogant, the frightened, the foolish, who think they can bring it about. Herod by executing John the Baptist, the Pharisees by opposing Jesus, the Roman authorities by crucifying him. But the Kingdom they wish to bring in by violence is the Kingdom they want, the Kingdom they perceive, the Kingdom which suits their own ends.

---

48. Isaiah 10: 5

That is the trouble with all dogmatism, with all authoritarianism, with all expressions of certainty. They know what the Kingdom is, they know how to achieve it. Thank God life is not like that. It is much more complex, many sided, subject to things we neither know nor understand.

Nevertheless, the vision which becomes delusion, the dogmatism, the authoritarianism which sees things in simplistic terms is very dangerous, as the Gore Vidal interpretation reveals. It was the dogmatism of Hitler which led to the gas chambers, the dogmatism of Stalin which led to extermination of millions, the arrogance of Boer which led to apartheid. The Christ comes to challenge all those who would take the Kingdom by violence for he brings the Kingdom not by violence but by love, by encounter, by healing, by searching, by suffering.

So what are we to say to the "Moral Majority" in America or elsewhere? What are we to say to those whose large visions threaten the world?

1. We must reject any form of literalistic understanding of scripture or any other (look at Islamic fundamentalism). What literalism really does is to enable us to read scripture or historic events from our own perspective, in our own way, and read into it the prejudices which we have and which reflect our own age. The prophet Ezekiel was not writing for a nuclear age but for a disobedient people. It is only careful critical study and analysis which can help us to see what scripture was saying in its own time and therefore what it may be saying to us. Any form of literalism or narrow traditionalism is destructive and selfish.

2. We need to be very wary of any person or group which claims too much authority for itself. True authority is something finely balanced, dispersed among many points and agencies, rests in consensus and is never absolute. True authority is what people see as authentic and which its very dispersal shares responsibility among many, not grabbed away by a few.

3. We need to acknowledge that there are many levels of meaning and understanding. At one level everything is simple, at another it is highly complex. I enjoy cooking. I can fling a few ingredients together and make a meal, quite simple, but don't ask me to examine or explain the chemical processes which are in operation. I don't understand them. Certainty, complete assurance, denies the complexities or reality and above all the mystery of God. False certainties remove the wonder, the mystery, the worship from God. Hence the Advent theme of the unexpected, the watching and the waiting for the God who comes in his own way, in his own time.

4. We do not engineer God's coming - this is his business. We are the John the Baptists. Our task is simply to make the way plain, to prepare the way, to prepare ourselves and the world around us in watchfulness, not putting ourselves at the centre but putting God at the centre. For there is always a check against the misuse and mis-appropriation of the Gospel for wrong and false ends. If it ends up in personal gain, personal aggrandisement, if it makes me smug and self-satisfied or makes me feel important, then we have to ask very seriously if it is the way and will of Christ. We do not know the manner of his coming but we do know what he brings and how he brings liberation, healing, sight to the blind - as in the Gospel today - and he brings it by way of the Cross.

Much modern 'successful' religion is a total perversion of this end and needs to be denounced. Gore Vidal is in this sense a true prophet.

If you have ears to hear, then hear.

Being the Church in the Third Millennium
A paper for the Christians in Public Life Programme
March 2000

It is often said today that people have not rejected Christianity, but they have rejected institutional religion. While Christianity expands on the worldwide scene, it is declining the Western world.[49] The tide of secularisation seems to be irresistible. The lack of a strong sense of community militates against the growth of community living, but it is what people are longing for. But has the institutional church ever been the thing that really mattered? Certainly we cannot do without it as a sign and a symbol of faith. But much more interesting things have always been found on the periphery of the organised Church.

On the margin
Let us take three examples of this 'peripheral Church' from three different periods: The *Devotio Moderna*, Early Methodism and Bonhoeffer's Theological College at Finkenwalde. The *Devotio Moderna*[50] (from which Thomas A Kempis' *Imitation of Christ* emerged) consisted of groups in the Rhineland who wanted to be real disciples of Jesus. They did not ignore the church, they went there for Mass and Confession, but they lived in community; shared the scriptures; examined the faith and worked out a way of life. They were the precursors of the Reformation, talking a language of priority and devotion.

The motivation of Early Methodism was to restore Scriptural Holiness to the Church. The development of the class system and groups of mutual support was similar to the *Devotio Moderna*.

The German Confessing Church needed to train new pastors and asked Bonhoeffer to organise this. His experience was described in his book *Life Together*.[51] A common life and sharing understandings of the gospel led to a way of life, which became a community of resistance in an oppressive society.

At the heart of the Christian faith lies a common sharing and a community grappling with what the story of Jesus means for them in their own situation. The four Gospels emerged out of a similar experience. The Church takes on new forms as people seek to discern a pattern of discipleship which relates to their own life and situation.

49. The formative reflections on this are in the writings of Fr. W Buhlmann, see especially *The Coming of the Third Church*, St. Paul Press 1976 and *Forward, Church!* St. Paul Press 1977
50. *Devotio Moderna* Basic writings, Ed. J. VanEngen, Paulist Press 1988
51. D. Bonhoeffer *Life Together* (1954)

The faith comes to life in an interaction between the Gospel and the world. This required realism and a toughness which is not always given to those who seek the solace of religion. Institutions are changed most effectively by oblique adaptation, not by deliberate design.

Beyond self-preservation

While there may be a decline in attendance in the mainstream churches, we live in an age where people are seeking meaning and identity in many other expressions of faith, from 'new age' to Eastern Religions. There is always a risk of the Church allowing itself to be captured in the culture of the age or of escaping into some nostalgic expression of faith. The Church of England has been in a state of crisis for most of the last century. The trauma of the First World War removed nearly all the accepted norms and assumption of the Church.[52] There has been a series of attempts to renew the structures in one way or another, from the *National Mission of Repentance and Hope* of 1917 through to the equally insignificant *Decade of Evangelism*. The wrong questions have been addressed. There has been a lack of trust that people can find their own way.

As Bonhoeffer saw very clearly, the motivation has been to seek the self-preservation of the institution. Christians must turn away from self-concern to a deep critical involvement with society. Just as the church needs to discern the Gospel for itself, so it must apply a critique of the Gospel to the world. We need to determine what to do and then find structures which will suit the task, not adapt old structures to a new task for which they are not fitted.

So what is the way ahead for the Church? It is called to be faithful to the Gospel and not to measure success by the standards used in a market-oriented society. Christians and people of good will need to sit down and seek to understand the Gospels. This should be done by taking seriously the findings of biblical scholarship. A faith which lacks rationality and avoids difficult intellectual questions will not command respect in our society. From such an understanding people will develop their own patterns of discipleship and seek support groups to enable them to try and fulfil it. Religious Communities and their Third Orders are a useful model[53] though such patterns of discipleship need to relate to the whole of life and not just to the personal dimension of it.

A new way of being Church

There is a role for new patterns of ministry which relates to

---

52. Alan Wilkinson, *The Church of England and the First World War*
53. See for example *The Rule for the Society of St John the Evangelist* (1987)

the whole area of human activity. The Pauline structure of 'Apostles, Prophets, Pastors, Evangelists and Teachers' may be helpful. So we could envisage a church consisting of many small groups with an overall strategy supervised by a Bishop or Apostle, who has oversight of an area is able to link groups with each other. This person would be assisted by one or two prophets, who would be trained to discern and comment on trends in society. Pastors, trained in pastoral care, could support the groups. Evangelists would seek to find way of commending the Gospel in society. Teachers who would be academically trained theologians and philosophers would help to provide an intellectual and theological undergirding for the life of the community. There will also be a need for Liturgists who provide meaningful rituals for modern society. Such a church would not be limited by present church division though it would need to have centres for major liturgical gatherings, for wider identity and meeting the needs of folk or implicit religion. Such a pattern would still need financial backing and a full-time ministry along the lines suggested above. Some national Church structure would be needed to relate to similar structures in our society and to engage with government and opinion-formers. There would also need to be the means of relating to worldwide ecclesiastical structures and to learn from and listen to what is happening in other societies, cultures and faiths.

This pragmatic approach avoids many of the issues relating to authority and tradition in the Church. At the same time if we faced up to the sort of Church which really relate to the world around us, we might well find that apparently intractable theological issues were put into a new perspective. Andrew Kirk is right to argue that in a pluriform society there will be pluriform expressions of the Church. One expression will be of communities and cells like that outlined above. Another will sit lightly in the Institution and seek to identify and interpret the signs of the Kingdom. A third will look toward Church planting, and another will work for the integration of these various approaches.

We need to go back to the Book of the Exodus. Here we see the people of Israel changing from slaves to a community. They formed different groups, doing different things, thereby forming the basis for a diverse society but governed by a common faith and law. Their society began with community groups which moved from slavery to become an institution. New life for the Church will come through a creative fragmentation, in search of new patterns of discipleship.

50th Anniversary of Ordination to the Priesthood
All Saints Convent, Oxford
13th June 2010

Luke 9: v.62:
No one who puts his hand to the plough and looks back is fit for the Kingdom of God.

These are strange occasions. About 11 years ago I was at a 40th anniversary celebration with David Burnside and as we came out of the Church he said to me: "That was a bit like a Requiem in advance". I hope this does not feel like that. I was not originally intending to preach, and asked Beau Stevenson to preach but he said: "No, people will want to hear you". So, being an obedient person, that is what I am doing.

Where does this text fit in? Jesus is calling his disciples to radical obedience, expressing what Bonhoeffer called *The Cost of Discipleship*. I have chosen this text because I wish to speak about five people who (apart from my close family) have been a deep influence on me.

The first of them is Bishop George Bell of Chichester. This was the text he preached on at my Confirmation on 24th March 1947 in the Lady Chapel of Chichester Cathedral. It has stuck with me ever since. Dennis Nineham once described Bishop Bell as "The greatest churchman of the 20th Century - not excluding William Temple". I have always wondered whether my commitment to ecumenism and my passionate devotion to the life and writings of Dietrich Bonhoeffer go back to that day in Chichester.

Not many years later, another priest came into my life in the shape of Christopher Heath, who was Chaplain of St Paul's School. A brilliant mathematician, he had taught as St Paul's since the 1920s and ordained in 1944. Just after he retired, the Oxford Examination Board gave him a dinner to mark his marking of A Level Maths papers for 50 years.

When I was 17, I went back to a Whitsunday Service at Chichester and returned convinced that I should be ordained. I told Chris Heath and he produced a notebook from his pocket and showed me where he had written a note that I was a potential ordinand sometime earlier. Although I was hopeless at Maths, he was the only master in the school who took any interest in my future. But that was not the end of our relationship, for after my first curacy, I became his curate in the Parish of St Mary Barnes. After my first vigorous but shy vicar, Chris was exactly

68

what I needed. He gave me a free hand. Not only did I promote things like jazz services, he enabled me to engage in creative dialogue with intelligent laity, following the publication of Robinson's *Honest to God*. Later he preached at my wedding. As a mathematician, his theology was more radical than he realised. He knew that mathematical models were like myths in the Bible, essential for their understanding. He was a kind, gracious man, who understood teenagers.

Then another even more influential figure came into my life. This was David Paton. I had met him once only a few years earlier, and then, out of the blue, he wrote and asked me if I would join him on the staff of the Missionary and Ecumenical Council of the Church Assembly. No one would dare call a Church organisation "MECCA" today! He may have had an exaggerated view of my abilities, but I had a very fruitful five years at Church House Westminster - servicing unity talks, assisting in theological dialogue, and working for the 1968 Lambeth Conference. It was meant to be the last Lambeth Conference, and it would have been much better if it had been! It was also at this time that I met Ruth, my wife, who was also working at Church House.

David was the son of William Paton, the pioneer ecumenist and a friend of George Bell. David had been a missionary in China, where he became convinced that the Communist revolution had more to do with the Gospel than what the missionaries had been doing. He had been editor of SCM Press and was a prophetic thinker who always spoke his mind, sometimes in a rather convoluted way. This led him to becoming a problem to the Church hierarchy. People were frightened to offer him a Deanery or Bishopric. He had turned down being Bishop of Hong Kong, hoping that a Chinaman would be appointed; instead an old colleague of David's got the job. He spent his last years as Rector of Gloucester, where he had a deep impact on the city's life. Both he and Michael Ramsey[54] had been pupils at Repton when Geoffrey Fisher was Headmaster, and they became good friends.

I must recount an event which took place at St John's Home just before Michael Ramsey died. It was after the Crockford affair[55] and David came to visit Michael. Just as David was leaving, Michael Ramsey said to him: "I thank God that I am no longer a member of the Church of England". I always kept in touch with David, and when he died I had to sort out his papers. He deserves a biography, which he has not had. He sustained me in my liberalism and radicalism.

54. Archbishop of Canterbury 1961 – 1974
55. For a contemporaneous account, see for example: http://www.nytimes.com/1987/12/09/world/oxford-theologian-tied-to-criticism-of-prelate-is-found-dead.html (accessed 29.05.17)

The next great figure in my life was Bishop Kenneth Skelton. He was Bishop of Lichfield when I went to work there, after my time in Headington. He was a quiet, shy man, who was valiant for the truth. He had been Bishop at Matabeleland at the height of the UDI, where he firmly resisted Ian Smith. He became known as "Red Skelton" and gained a CBE for his participation in the Tiger Talks which helped to resolve the difficult situation there. He was perceptive, sharp and compassionate. Our friendship continued until after he retired to Sheffield. I preached at his wife's funeral and at an amazing occasion when he celebrated the 60th anniversary of his ordination and the 40th anniversary of his consecration as a Bishop. When he died, I arranged his funeral in Lichfield Cathedral. We read excerpts from his great address to the Christian Council of Rhodesia, where he quoted Herbert Butterfield: 'Commit yourself to Christ, and for the rest be totally uncommitted.'[56] He made a deep impact on me.

There are others I could speak of and you are all here because you too have been part of my path of discipleship, but the last person I have to speak of deeply influenced me far more than all the others, from 1955 right through to his death thirty years later. That was Christopher Bryant. He has been described by Father Campbell (who sadly died yesterday), as: "the greatest Father Superior the Cowley Fathers never had". A Jungian psychologist with gentle but firm insights, he was my spiritual director for so long that we became close friends. Sydney Evans, preaching as his funeral said that Christopher saw himself as engaged in a "threefold dialogue":

- With the Gospel.
- With the Christian spiritual tradition whereby Christianity relates to a changing world.
- With the finest minds of our age, like Darwin, Marx and Jung.

This dialogue emerged from deep contemplative prayer. To this day, I make little pilgrimages to Rose Hill Cemetery, where his ashes are buried. He was a major figure for my growth and learning in the faith, but so were all the others.

And what do they have in common? They were all people who never gave up.

---

56. Butterfield, H. (1957) *Christianity and History*, p.189

- George Bell's fearless pursuit of Christian Unity, and risking losing popularity through his attacks on the indiscriminate bombing during the Second World War in the House of Lords.
- Chris Heath, simply being a faithful, insightful Pastor who trusted people.
- David Paton, totally honest about himself and others, regardless of the consequences.
- Kenneth Skelton, facing persecution and unpopularity. Standing firm and giving others confidence.
- Christopher Bryant, whose life had two parts. For many years a faithful monk and then later, having had a deep change of mind, becoming a powerful writer and teacher.

No one who puts his hand to the plough and looks back is fit to enter the Kingdom of God.

I am not worthy of these people, nor am I worthy of your friendship and support, but I still try to follow these Gospel words, given to me by George Bell. None of these people will be aware of their influence on me. How they gave me a wider vision of the church, a greater trust in God's people and a deeper commitment. Thankfully, none of us are aware of the effects our actions have on others. In his introduction to Bonhoeffer's book *The Cost of Discipleship*, Bell picks out one sentence from Bonhoeffer which sums it all up: 'When Jesus calls a man, He bids him come and die'.

That is what discipleship and ministry are all about, however inadequately we live up to it.

On the dedication of a memorial window to Norman Moses
Sermon preached at St Ignatius, Hendon
St Luke's Day 1998

Luke 22: v. 28:
You have stood firmly by me in my times of trial

I have a grandson called Ignatius. I am not sure if he is aware of the origins of his name. He is only six, and prefers to be called "Iggy", but at some point I shall need to tell him of his famous namesakes - Ignatius of Antioch, after whom this Church is named. He was also known as "Theophorus" meaning "carried by God" or "the God Bearer". But there is also St Ignatius Loyola, that profound founder of the Jesuits, whose *Spiritual Exercises* have become such a vital part of the spiritual growth of so many people. St Ignatius of Antioch was an early martyr - almost too eagerly a martyr.

My text is from St Luke's Gospel. St Luke, whose day it is today, has a distinctive view of the nature of Christian discipleship. This is clear from these words uttered in the context of the Last Supper. Jesus says to his disciples *You are those who have continued with me in my trials.* This is a way of describing the nature of Christian discipleship. It is his trials that will lead Jesus into crucifixion and death and the way to new life and hope. St Ignatius was very bothered about heretics called 'Docetists'. They believed that Jesus has not died on the cross but only appeared to die. Reflecting on his own situation Ignatius wrote 'If he suffered in mere appearance why am I in bonds?'

No the way of discipleship is indeed to share in Christ's sufferings: to be carried along by God in His pain. Otherwise there is no hope.

We are here today to dedicate a window to St Luke in memory of Father Norman Moses. The last time I was in this Church was just under two years ago for his funeral. In his years of patient ministry, Norman only had two curates: the first was Harry Hindmarch who worked with him at St Jude's South Shields. He ended up as Canon and Rural Dean in the Southwark Diocese, where I got to know him.

Harry died many years ago and I was the other curate. It is hard to think that I left St Aidan's in October 1961, thirty-seven years ago.

I have chosen my text because I think it is an insight into Norman's life and ministry. Very much a Sunderland person, educated at Bede Grammar School, the only time he left County Durham was to train for the priesthood at Kings College London (as did some others here today). I rarely saw him without his KCL scarf. He, like St Ignatius, saw his role a sharing in Christ's life and suffering. He was in many ways a shy and self-effacing man, which made it difficult for them to get to know him. He was a deeply caring and patient man, who visited endlessly and prayed frequently. So he built up his ministry with deep persistence, patience and caring.

Two parishes dominated his ministry. St Jude's South Shields, which he served for fourteen years and St Aidan's Grangetown, which he served for nineteen years. But I suspect that in some ways St Ignatius held his heart from his childhood and, in retirement he returned here.

Here was a caring, self-effacing, devout, shy man who sought above all to live in Christ and with Christ. He also cared deeply about the ordering of worship and the beauty of churches. He had an uncanny knack of extracting money from people. Here too, was someone with a close-knit family, which was much given to hospitality, in the way that everyone expects in this part of the world. It is good to see his devoted sister, Marjorie, and other members of her family here today.

The Church of England has undergone dramatic and almost drastic changes since the 1940s when Norman was ordained, and the way the full-time priesthood now operates and is understood is very different from the way he was trained. For Norman, his model was the Cure d'Ars, that quiet priest who gave himself fully to Christ and the community and who exercised a deep ministry of love. I am not sure who is the model for the clergy today. It does seem to me that the style of ministry which Norman and his contemporaries exercised, and from which we learned, is not one which is predominant today. It was a life nurtured in prayer, and enabling people to be themselves. It was serving, caring and self-effacing. How often did I hear Norman say that the Cross is "I crossed out", for the meaning of JOY was "Jesus first, Others second and Yourself last".

Christian discipleship does not consist in promoting oneself or in marketing, meeting one's needs or seeking self-fulfilment. But that is the culture of today's world and it has permeated the ministry as well. No - the way of discipleship is to continue with Christ in his trials.

So Norman's pattern of ministry and ours has to be a way of protest against the greed, selfishness and individualism of our time. It is a protest that comes not in words but also in a simple lifestyle, a daily routine of prayer and sacraments, in hospitality and caring and in building up family life. But it is above all continuing with Christ in his trials, which was one of St Luke's great insights. It was one which motivated St Ignatius. For the Kingdom does not grow by great acts of power; it does not grow through publicity campaigns; it does not grow by going with the crowd. It grows through patient love and caring, through a life lived out in seeking God in ways that are often quiet and hidden. Thus it has more chance to develop, naturally and easily. These are the sorts of lessons I, and many others, learned from Norman Moses and we are glad to remember him and to continue with Christ in his trials.

I hope it is a lesson which my grandson, Ignatius, will one day be able to learn and then to be prouder of his name.

The Time of Religionless Christianity has come?

Holland House

30 May 2008

The great Jewish philosopher Martin Buber once remarked that 'religion is the enemy of humanity'[57] and if we look around the world today, we can see plenty of examples of the destructive effects of religion. Fundamentalist Christianity in America destroys many people's lives and is a factor both in relation to the tensions between Israel and Palestine and in the Iraq war. Wahhabist Islam with its desire to create a worldwide Caliphate and the imposition of Sharia law on everybody is another example, and we could go on. But first we need to define our terms very carefully.

The phrase 'Religionless Christianity' became a popular concept in the 1960s but it owes it origins to Bonhoeffer's *Letters and Papers from Prison* where, writing to his friend Eberhart Bethge, Bonhoeffer outlined a future for Christianity. What lay behind it was his realisation, like Buber, that the Bible is an immensely this-worldly book. There is not a category to be put into a slot called "Religion" whereas in fact God is at the heart of everything.

Look at Psalm 139:

> *Where can I escape from your Spirit?*
> *Where can I flee from your presence?*
> *If I climb up into heaven you are there*
> *If I take my bed in Sheol you are there*
> *Or if I travel to the limits of the east*
> *Or dwell in the Bounds of western sea*
> *Even there your hand will be guiding me.*
> *Your right hand can hold me fast.*

Or reflect on Christ's promise to *be with you always to the ends of the earth*[58] or of the affirmation in Epistle to the Hebrews that *Jesus Christ is the same yesterday, today, and forever*[59] or the assertion of the Letter to the Colossians that *in God all things exist and are held together.* The key concept in Biblical religion is that of *Shalom:* wholeness, integrity and peace, not

---

57 Quoted in Lash (1988) Easter in Ordinary: Reflections on Human Experience and the Knowledge of God
58. Matthew 28: v. 20
59. Hebrews 13: v. 8

of a division into different categories. This is the God of religionless Christianity.

Christ is at the centre, so Bonhoeffer wrote in his letters 'Jesus does not call us to new religion but to life'. This led him to pose the question 'What is the significance of a Church in a religionless world?' But we now have a world which is not religionless but in many ways over-religious. However, it is important to examine what Bonhoeffer meant by religion. His biographer, Eberhart Bethge said that what Bonhoeffer meant by religion was the following:

1. *An expression of excessive individualism, which cuts you off from others, and encourages us to abandon the world.* We need to remember that he was acting again the neo-Paganism of Hitler's Germany. These days, we see quite a bit of this in new Age Spirituality, which seems to be an escape from the world. Bonhoeffer was fighting against the trappings of Nazism as a classic example of unchristian religion.

2. *God is seen as outside the world rather than at the heart of it.* This leads us to divide the world into two realms - the sacred and the secular, the spiritual and the material. But in the Bible and in Christ, these two are one. It makes a distinction between Biblical religion and non-Biblical religion. Non-Biblical religion is the religion of salvation out of this world. Biblical religion is that of redemption within history. We see in this the roots of Latin American Liberation theology; redemption is going on now, in history, in reconciliation, in healing, in actions for justice and in peace. This could be seen as a response to the Marxist analysis of religion as the opium of the people. People put up with the miseries of this world because of what will happen in the next. (So the Islamic bombers will be offered 72 virgins in the next - not much use if we do not have bodies). But we need also note John Kent's stricture that if religion was the opium of the people, then not many people were addicted to it.

3. *Religion tends to divide.* It becomes one sector and thus a relic of the past. But God cannot be only part. God is all and in all.

4. *Religion for Bonhoeffer had a sense of Deus ex machina.* God is there to provide the answer to things which we do not understand.

Religion is sort of a spiritual chemist's shop. There was a time at the height of the Parish Communion Movement when people talked about going to Communion on Sundays to get a 'top up' for the week. It turned the Church and God into a sort of petrol station. But this is a blasphemy; we can't 'use' God. This is a 'God of gaps' to escape into, or an explanation of things which we do not understand. Dean Inge had perceived this fifty years earlier when he wrote 'Those who take refuge in gaps find themselves in a very tight corner when the gaps begin to close.'[60] In a way, this is the sort of religion which Richard Dawkins is attacking and from this point of view he is right. But he cannot seem to be able to grasp that this is not the sort of God most of us believe in. I do not believe in the God that Dawkins does not believe in.

5. *Religion is related to privilege.* It is the luxury of the cultured classes and a sign of superiority, rather than dignifying humanity. Hence Bonhoeffer's famous remark that 'only those who cry out for the Jews may sing Gregorian chants.' Life has to have integrity and integration.

So, religion which splits life into compartments, sees God as an answer to what we do not understand, which fails to keep life whole, is a denial of Christianity. That is why we need Religionless Christianity.

Two other aspect of Bonhoeffer's thought helps to make this clear. One is the concept of 'Jesus Christ, the man for others.' As Christ died for us, so we, both as individuals and as a Church must live for others. There can be no sense of Church living to itself or seeking self-preservation. That is what I see around me today, expressed in phrases like 'a mission-shaped Church' or 'fresh expressions' which seem to me to be simply devices to preserve the institution. No; whoever will save his life must lose it.

The other is the need for what Bonhoeffer called the secret discipline (the *Disciplina Arcana*). He explains much of this in his book Life Together. The discipline has to be God-centred and community-centred by people sharing their own and each other's faith through prayer, common worship, meditation and confession. Religionless Christianity does not abolish prayer or worship, rather it is re-orienting it. It is through its discipline that the Church engages with the God who lies at the heart of all things. Thus, in Bethge's words, 'If the Church

60. W.R. Inge, 'Conclusion', p. 366 in Needham (ed.), (1925) *Science, Religion and Reality*

cannot relate to the secularised world in such a way that its existence in the world's life can be immediately seen, the Church had better keep silent. True life comes through prayer and righteous action.'

If then the time for Religionless Christianity has come, what sort of Church should we expect to be in?

One that rejects those things which divide and separate, are triumphalistic, divisive, judgemental, rejecting the world or humanity. Much of today's popular religions of many faiths can be seen like that, but we have to take care in this not to become too judgemental ourselves.

We have to take account of what the historians and the sociologists are saying to us about the present state of European Religions. (The situation in Africa and in the USA is utterly different, but I suspect will end up being much the same). We have witnessed what Callum Brown has called *The Death of Christian Britain*. [2009]. We have seen what Grace Davie has defined as *Believing without Belonging* (1994): and alongside these two things we have seen and are witnessing what the Australian David Tacey has called *The Spirituality Revolution* (2004).

The first two may be more familiar to you than the Third. Brown's first book defined things too narrowly, but he demonstrated clearly that there was a dramatic decline in the role of institutional religion in Britain after 1963 (he is precise as that). Grace Davie finds many people having some sort of residual faith but not seeing how it relates to the institution. Tacey, by working with his students in Melbourne, affirmed what others have found that very few people are without some sort of spiritual experiences in their lives but they do not relate this to the Church or any other religion. The reactions of the Churches to this, he says, has been of two sorts. One has been to try and assert the Christian tradition over people's experiences. The other has been the assertion of fundamentalism that, he says, 'provides pre-packaged answers to the questions, which people are not asking. This will lead to more religious fanaticism and intolerance until we can bring our religious life into the open and express the non-rational forces that underpin it.'

So we have to realise (and I suspect Bonhoeffer knew this) that while the Church has retained the forms of institutional Christianity, it has lost the substance of it. This has happened because it has failed to remain engaged with its surrounding culture. So Tacey writes that 'the old religious view fails to resonate with the understandings of the young or the secular world in which they live. Western religion will have to recognise that we need to have much of our religion translated into modern terms and linked to everyday life situations.' He points out that religious conservatives are sure that they are conserving tradition by refusing to make way for the new, but they are destroying the tradition they profess to love. Real tradition has to be open to the inwardness and spiritual meaning found outside the Church. He sums it up by quoting Picasso: "Tradition is having a baby, not wearing your grandfather's hat."

But all this is not to say that there are no signs of hope. There are many small groups loosely attached to the Church who are trying to work out a faith and a spirituality for this secular world which are connected to religious communities, like the Jesuit Christian life Communities, or people who are members of third orders of religious communities, or those like the Iona Community. But I do not see in many places the real willingness to the committed, deep hard work which will be required to bring this about. It is no easy task. The Australian Jesuit Fr. Gittins has put it like this, 'Institutions as such are inherently conservative. Individuals or small groups are more likely to be on the edge; cutting or otherwise. And individuals or small groups who follow Jesus are faithful and radical disciples first and only incidentally members of institutions.'[61]

I think that is quite near what I mean by Religionless Christianity. Bonhoeffer reflected from his prison cell on what the Church of the future will be like. He wrote:

The Church is the Church only when it exists for others. To make a start it should give away all its property to those in need. The clergy must lie solely on the free will offerings of the congregations or engage in secular callings. The Church must share in the secular problems of ordinary human life not dominating but helping and serving. It must tell men of every calling what it means to live in Christ, to exist for others.

We can see many of these things happening now and it was Moltmann in *The Open Church* (1978) who saw that as the Church was stripped of its trappings in a secular world, it was more free to be itself and to be real disciples.

It is a call to be Christ like, open and vulnerable and I suspect the world will force us into it. There was a cry in the 1960s that "The world sets the agenda for the Churches." Many criticised this, partly because most Christians have an inadequate theology of the world but also because it failed to see that it may be God speaking through the

---

61. A.J. Gittins (1999) *Reading the Clouds*

world who is setting the agenda. So Religionless Christianity is a call to the Church to become more Christlike, to be weak and vulnerable.

As David Bosch puts it:

> Only if we turn our backs in false power and false security can there be authentic Christian mission. True hope is hope in the midst of adversity, and yet anchored in God's coming triumph over his rebellious world.

This is Religionless Christianity: open, vulnerable and weak. Bonhoeffer summed it up in *The Cost of Discipleship*:

> Amid poverty and suffering, hunger and thirst, they are meek and peacemakers, persecuted and scorned by the world, although it is for their sake alone that the world is allowed to continue, and it is they who protect the world from the wrath and judgement of God. They are strangers and sojourners on earth. They seek those things that are above not the things that are on the earth. For their future life is yet to be made manifest but hidden with Christ in God. Although they are visible to society, they are always unknown even to themselves, looking only to their Lord.

That is the Church for Others, this is Religionless Christianity. Never have we needed it more than now.

Thanksgiving Service for the Restoration of the Cathedral

Sermon at Worcester Cathedral

25th September 2011

I Corinthians 3: v. 10 :
According to the grace of God given to me, like a master builder I laid a foundation and someone else is building on it. Each builder must choose with care how to build on it.

There is an old story about someone who met a road sweeper and he asked him how long he had been doing the job. "For over forty years," he replied.

"Then you must have gone through a lot of brooms doing that" was the response.

"Oh no!" said the sweeper. "I have had the same broom all the time. It has had four new brushes and three new handles, but it is still the same broom."

As with brooms, so with our bodies and so with buildings, replacing themselves all the time. It's a natural process.

Now, the story of this building is similar. Over the centuries, the building has been restored many times and very little of the original remains. Wulfstan wept when he replaced his old Anglo-Saxon Cathedral with the new Romanesque one in 1087. In the twelfth century there were two very bad fires and in 1202, Wulfstan's Cathedral was burned down and restored over the next two centuries. Much of this was inspired by the canonisation of St Wulfstan and by the burial of King John. His son, Henry III poured vast resources into the rebuilding and re-ordering of the building. These ongoing repairs came from Royal endowments, from monastic lands, and a Royal Charter for the monks to hold an annual fair; and then later by a considerable income from pilgrims visiting the shrines of St Oswald, St Wulfstan and Our Lady of Worcester. (It is interesting to note that when the ten foot high statue of Our Lady was disrobed and finally destroyed at the Reformation it was discovered to be the statue of a man!).

Worcester was a model run for Henry VIII's dissolution of monasteries, and the last Prior became the first Dean and some of the monks became Canons. So the building survived the Reformation, but it was badly desecrated in the Civil War. Horses were stabled here, windows were smashed, the organ torn down and the separate Bell

Tower in College Yard demolished, with bad results in later years.[62]

At the Restoration of the Monarchy (1660) the Chapter started services again and many repairs were carried out, as they were in the next century. It is at this point that we discover the key to the Cathedral's problems, when we find that the soft sandstone was being tied together with metal sandstone. (Here is one which I have kept). So, in the nineteenth century, a massive restoration had to take place. The architect had warned that if the work was not done, the Music meeting (e.g. the Three Choirs Festival) could not take place. The Dean, John Peel, was the brother of the Prime Minister, and was well connected. He used to be carried around the streets of Worcester in a sedan chair, from which he waved to the crowds.

The restoration was the largest and most expensive of any cathedral in England in the 19th Century, totalling then to £114,295.11s and 3p. Whole walls were replaced, new flooring and new furnishings provided, but even so, some work was left uncompleted (like the West wall of the South Transept). Two major benefactors and fundraisers were Lord Lyttleton and the Earl of Dudley, for which they have memorials in the Lady Chapel. The Earl of Dudley donated £5,000 for the restoration of the Tower so that it could have one of the finest ring of bells in the country.

The work began in 1866 and was completed in 1874. There were major thanksgiving events, lasting three days. Singers from St George's Windsor, Christ Church Oxford, Eton College and both Hereford and Gloucester Choirs augmented the Cathedral choir. Following the opening service, dignitaries were entertained to a lavish lunch in College Hall.[63]

Thereafter, many Deans made their mark in different ways. Dean Moore Ede put in the windows in the cloister made from Gateshead glass. Dean Davies suffered by being here during the war when Prince Arthur's Chantry was bricked up, and Dean Milburn took a great interest in the fabric. By the 1970s it was clear that more work needed doing. A pinnacle fell through the roof, the heating needed improving and Dean Kemp set up a fundraising Trust, which we were able to revive later. Dean Baker restored and greatly improved the Crypt. But worse was being revealed. In the 1980s a large piece of stone fell from the Choir roof just before a service. The then architect, Bernard Ashwell stood on the tower roof when the bells were ringing and sensed far more

62. Ute Engel's *Worcester Cathedral, An Architectural History* (2007) summarises the restoration history. See also Stanford E. Lehmberg's *Cathedrals under Siege 1600- 1700*
63. See P Barratt *Barchester: English Cathedral Life in the Nineteenth Century*. (1993)

movement than there should have been. Similarly, he found that the effects of removal of some pinnacles in previous years was now to push the walls out.

So when Kenneth Wiltshire was appointed architect, the Chapter knew a major restoration was needed, and it was very major. The Central Tower was in real danger of collapsing (though not everyone believed it), and specialist engineering techniques had to be used. Kenneth was very worried that there might be an earthquake. People dismissed it. But only just after the work was completed, there was a small earthquake which affected us in the Deanery. But there was more than the Tower. The effects of the metal clamps cracking stone were being seen all over the building. Fortunately, Kenneth Wiltshire, to whom we owe an enormous debt, costed the work properly. So we knew what were in for, and twenty years later, the restoration (wisely supervised by his successor Chris Romain) has come in almost exactly on the original estimates. A strategy slowly evolved, to do the work ourselves by increasing the work staff, training stonemasons and thus saving us VAT. We should today express our gratitude to the work staff, who, over twenty years, have done such a magnificent job.

A brand new Dean, who knew no one, was faced with problems, but was greatly blessed with real help and good will. Bishop Philip Goodrich used his contacts vigorously. Sir Thomas Dunne, the Lord Lieutenant, gave me some extremely wise and discreet advice. Mr Richard Pugh, well known for his charitable works in Worcester used his contacts and chaired a very happy and well working committee. The Trustees looked after the money well, benefiting from the 15% interest rates for a time! We were very pleased to have Lord Leonard Wolfson, an old Vigornian, who had a great interest in King John, as our patron. Mr. Cecil Duckworth helped build the workshops. The fundraisers Everald Compton, who had completed a successful appeal at Ely, were brought in. They told us we would raise the first four million pounds in two and a half years in 9,000 donations and then we committed ourselves to raising an extra £300,000 every year thereafter. We would not have done it if English Heritage Grants had not become available. A key person whose work needs very public acclamation was Mrs. Jean Armstrong who, through her Secretaryship of the Three Choirs Festival, knew many people and worked tirelessly on the Appeal. A main element was the daily meetings she and I had together. The Chapter and Colin Wilson, the Steward, acted as one and we were determined not to let up at all until we got there. In this, we were helped with a generous donation of

£400,000 from the Diocesan Board of Finance. This bound the Cathedral and the Diocese together and we responded by committing ourselves to pay an annual quota to the Diocese, like every other church.[64]

I laid a foundation and someone else is building on it. Paul is talking about handing on the faith and building it up. In this process, we rely on each other and so the heritage is passed on.

But what are Cathedrals for? In 2000, I took a sabbatical leave and looked at the organisation and administration of 26 Cathedrals in the Anglican Communion and discovered a lot of surprising things. But English cathedrals have a distinctive place, sometimes unwisely copied in other cultures.[65]

For some Worcester Cathedral is that dark and gloomy place at the end of the High Street. But if they venture inside, they find the history of the community, a focus for civic and national events and something to inspire. It has been a great preaching centre and a place for great music and the arts. But is that enough to justify their maintenance?

In a secular nation, it is a paradox that cathedrals are more valued now than they have ever been. They give us our history, but they also give us a sense of mystery and glory. The Normans civilised this country through castles and cathedrals often built next to each other. They were expressions of power and dominance, but they can also be centres of service, caring and acceptance in a wider community.

At the Reformation, Henry VIII kept cathedrals to be centres of learning and education. We need them for our humanity, because they remind us of what we are, people who know our place under the reign of God, and so we have the right priorities. Cathedrals make us stop and think, reflect on the meaning of life and to reach out beyond ourselves. I recall quoting Robert Browning at my Installation, 'A man's reach should exceed his grasp, or what's a heaven for?'

If ongoing maintenance work is continued, we may not need another major restoration. Much could be done through your support, through regular giving and legacies. If the earlier restorations had not taken place, there would be no Cathedral for us to restore. After 20 years of restoration, we can thank God for all that he has done and achieved. We can build on those who came before us, and we can make the future grateful to us by ensuring that this great building will be sustained for them.

I laid a foundation and someone else is building on it.

64 I expanded in this in a paper for the Deans' Conference entitled *A Case Study of Fundraising – Worcester Cathedral 1992*

65. Jeffery, R. (2002) *Cathedrals Around the World*, annual report for the Friends of Christ Church

Paul saw the church like a human body, which renews itself from time to time. We are not really talking just about bricks and mortar. The cathedral is an expression of people's desire for God, and of humanity reaching out to express the glory and the mystery of God. The fabric may not be the same, but the purpose, the expression, history and the glory are the same. It is the same broom after over a thousand years.

May I end on a more personal note? It is exactly 15 years since I last preached here. My time as Dean (as strangely with some Deans before me), was overtaken by a personal tragedy. It has not made it easy to be here today, but it gives me the chance to thank all those who have given me and my family friendship and support since the sudden death of my wife sixteen years ago. I never enter this place without being reminded of her funeral. That event changed our lives in many ways. Many of you have been good friends and propped us up. That is a small, personal illustration of what cathedrals mean to people, bringing together the past, the present and the future to the Glory of God, and we need to keep it that way.

All of them became drowsy and slept

A sermon given at All Saints Convent
6th November 2011

Matthew 25: v. 5:
All of them became drowsy and slept.

If we take a detached view of what we do in our lives, it will not be long before we realise that sleeping must take up about one third of our lives. So at the age of 75 we will have spent 25 years asleep. We don't often think of it that way, but it is the case.

Sleep, however, remains a bit of a mystery and there are many problems attached to sleep. May people have deeply disturbed sleep, some people go sleepwalking, others disturb their partners by excessive snoring. (I occasionally wake myself up with my own snoring!). But there are now sleep clinics where some of these problems can be sorted out. We know that sleep goes through various phases, some of light and some of it very deep. But we all know what happens if we lack sleep. We get irritable, we get tired, we can't concentrate. It is an essential part of living. It is a subject that has exercised many poets.

Shakespeare speaks of 'sleep that knits up the ravelled sleeve of care'[66] and of 'to sleep, perchance to dream.'[67]

It is rather strange that St. Matthew, who lays great store by dreams seems to have a very negative view of sleep. Sleeping is seen as laziness. The thief comes while people are asleep; the disciples fall asleep while Jesus prays in Gethsemane. A child thought to be dead is simply sleeping.

Today's parable has posed many problems for the commentators. It is maybe a Jewish story that has been adapted but it seems very strange that the attendants are expected to wait for the bridegroom to come in the middle of the night. The early Church seems to have adapted it to equate the bridegroom with Jesus and the need to be ready for his coming whenever that may be. John van Ruysbroek, the 14th century Flemish mystic centres his whole book *The Adornment of the Spiritual Marriage* on this passage. He lays great weight on the need to be prepared for the arrival of the bridegroom.

The announcement of the arrival in the middle of the night seems to imply the end of the world.

---

66. *Macbeth*, Act 2, Scene 3
67. *Hamlet*, Act 3, Scene 1

The Bible in general seems a bit ambivalent about sleep. God makes Adam sleep so he can create Eve.

The psalmist says that sleep is a gift from God, who never sleeps. Sleep is often linked to dreams of spiritual significance, like Jacob wrestling with the angel and Joseph having dreams to foretell the future.

But the Bible seems to imply that sleep is something to escape from. *Awake thou that sleepest and arise from the dead and Christ will give you light.*[68] It is as if it is only unredeemed humanity who sleeps.

Sleep is also linked with death. Sleep is in a sense a form of death. Those who die, sleep with their fathers. John Donne took this very literally and slept in his coffin every night to prepare for death.

But if sleep is so essential to us that we spend a third of our lives asleep, there must be more than this. In most things there is a positive as well as negative side. We need rest and refreshment. Today's Gospel does not condemn sleep, but condemns those who are not prepared, who are not ready. Shelley has an interesting line:

Some say that gleams of a remoter world
Visit the soul in sleep - that death is slumber
And that it shapes the busy thoughts outnumber
Of those who wake and live.[69]

One of the functions of sleep seems to be to enable us to assimilate all that has happened in the previous day and to order our minds. This is very important in an age when everybody expects things to be instant. The other more positive side is shown in the Office of Compline, familiar to many of us, which calls us to lay down in sleep and take our rest. *For it is thou Lord only that makest us dwell in safety.*[70] That's nearer to the point. Sleep is an expression of trust in God.

We learn to rest in His hands. We know we can rest in peace *for underneath are the everlasting arms.*[71] He gives his beloved sleep, so that we can arise and go out and meet the bridegroom.

So sleep is not negative. It is yet another opportunity to meet with Christ. To do what we always need to do – to place ourselves in God's hands, morning, noon and night and so meet him in sleeping as well as in waking.

So sleeping is yet another picture of what life is all about.

---

68. Ephesians 5: v. 14
69. III from *Mont Blanc*, Percy Bysshe Shelley
70. Psalm 4, v. 9
71. Deuteronomy 22: v 27

Letting God do with us what He wills.

The 17th century writer Sir Thomas Browne put it like this:

Sleep is fine, so like death I dare not trust it without my prayers.[72]

So from this perspective sleep is a spiritual exercise whereby we learn to die to ourselves and live to Christ. There can be nothing negative about sleep, for it brings us nearer to God.

---

72. Sir Thomas Browne (1605 – 1682): *An evening prayer*, available at http://www. bartleby.com/296/108. html (accessed 29.05.17)

Morning Glory
A sermon given at Christ Church, Oxford
30 April 2000

Psalm 143: v. 8:
In the morning let me know of thy love for I put my trust in you.
Isaiah 26: v. 9:
At dawn I seek for you
Luke 24: v. 1:
Very early on the first day of the week they came to the tomb.

There is a real sense in which desire and longing are linked with the morning, just as every morning is like a new creation. Some people find it easy to get up in the morning, and others find it very difficult. My wife and I were complete opposites in this direction and there was one day when we hit the jackpot and she came to bed just as I was getting up!

The morning, like Easter, is a symbol of new beginning, a new hope, a new start and I suppose anyone who is not a total pessimist believes deep down that each day will provide a new beginning, that renewal and new life is just around the corner. That presumably is part of the Easter hope and it is what keeps us going. There must be a sense in which the older you get; the more you appreciate the morning and what it might bring.

Dylan Thomas, in *Poem On his Birthday* puts it like this:

That the closer I move
To death, one man through his sundered bulks,
The louder the sun blooms
And the tusked, ramshackling sea exults;
And every wave of the way
And gale I tackle, the whole world of them
With more triumphant faith
Than ever was since the world was said
Spins its morning of praise.[73]

Yes, the older one is, the more we need both mornings of praise and more triumphant faith. Today I reach the landmark of becoming a pensioner. Also this year I have been priest of the Church for forty years, and I begin to rejoice more in the mornings but also hope for new dawns.

---

73. p.170, Thomas, D. (1952) *Collected poems*, London: J.M.Dent

Nineteen years ago my great friend and teacher, Canon David Paton, asked me to preach for him on the occasion of his 40th anniversary of priesting and I have dug out the sermon to see what I said. I pointed out how the clerical profession was changing and tried to tackle a question raised by Canon Frank Wright when he asked: 'Where are those *pastores pastorum* who will unlock for us this treasury of the grace of God, and allow those gifts to flow freely?'[74]

It is a proper question. But today I would pose it in a wider context. We are familiar with the image of the priest as the cork in the bottle stifling the bubbling life of Christ, which cannot get out. But today I would want to pose it in terms of where we can find expressions of Church, which will allow the treasury of God's grace to flow freely. Where can the freedom, the humanity, the excitement, and the expectancy of an Easter faith be seen? Where is the new dawn for faith? Not that faith has vanished, not that there are not remarkable examples of faith all around us, but things seem to be stifled and restricted. It is as if the tomb has not opened.

The history of the church is full of attempts to renew the Church and make it more relevant. Some have been more effective; some have been more radical than others. The cry *'ecclesia semper reformanda'* has much to be said for it. We are always in a process of change and renewal and if we are not, the life has gone out of us. Anyone who has heard me preach more than about three times will know that I have a passionate devotion to the writings of Dietrich Bonhoeffer. This is not just a fad; it is because without his insights I very much doubt whether I would have remained within the Christian community at all. In his *Letters and Papers from Prison*, he describes the sort of Church he expected to see emerge out of the post-world war situation. He was passionately concerned that the Church had got caught up in a process of self-preservation rather than being the community of the disciples of Christ. In an outline for a book, which he never wrote, he expressed his view like this:

> The church is only the church when it exists for others. To make a start it should give away all its property to those in need. The clergy must live solely on the free will offerings of their congregations or possibly engage in some secular calling. The church must share in the secular problems of ordinary human life, not dominating, but helping and serving. It must tell men of every calling what it means to live in Christ, to exist for others. In particular, our own church will have to take the field against

74. p. 84, Wright, F. (1980) *The pastoral nature of the ministry*, London: SCM Press

the vices of hubris, power worship, envy and humbug, as the roots of all evil. It will have to speak of moderation, purity, trust, and modesty. It must not underestimate the importance of human example; it is not abstract argument, but example, that gives its word emphasis and power. Further; the question of revising the creeds (the Apostles' creed); revision of Christian apologetics; reform of the training for the ministry and the pattern of clerical life.

Now that is not the Church you or I belong to. It might be better if it was. Bonhoeffer was right to expect that the way the institution operates should itself be expressive of the Gospel. Worldly power, self-preservation, and personal domination are not expressive of the gospel. Too easily the Church gives the impression that it possesses the Gospel. Popular hymns like 'We have a Gospel to proclaim' make me squirm. The church and the clergy do not possess the Gospel. They should be seeking to allow the Gospel to possess them. But just as Christians should expect sinners to sin, so any reading of the Bible should lead us to expect institutional religion to become self-concerned. That is one of the main messages of the Old Testament. Yet it is an essential part of human nature that we need and have to have institutional structures. We cannot operate without them but they must not dominate us.

In my forty-one years of ministry I have put a great deal of effort into trying to see how the Church might really be a church for others. I have spent hours working with radical groups for renewal. I have committed myself to really hard work for the ecumenical movement. I have spent even more hours working in committees, Board, Commissions and Synods of the Church of England. What I have witnessed is a church turning increasingly in on itself. I suspect that I have wasted a great deal of God's time in the process. I now find myself very out of sympathy with much that the Church of England is doing, with its centralisation, pseudo-management structures and lack of prophetic voice to the Nation. I long for that new dawn and that new morning when not only individual Christians but the corporate church is really washing the feet of humanity and living out a self-emptying life for the world.

I think I now see where is has gone wrong. We went head on at trying to change the Church, instead of ourselves. We thought that structural change would bring about effective change. That has been the motivation behind the creation of the Archbishop's Council and all that has gone along with it. The history of the church actually shows that it is as groups of Christians try to work out and live out their own pattern of discipleship that the institution adapts and bends and changes as a consequence. Effective change takes place incidentally. It does not come about by direct determined effort. We do indeed need enablers who will unlock the rich treasury of God's Grace, but those enablers have to follow the way of the Cross. We have to realise that we have to be open, vulnerable, weak, nothing, so that Christ may act in us. As soon as we claim power and are sure that we know what the answers are we undermine the Gospel.

Yet there is no need for despair. All around me I find encouragement from those who have caught a glimpse of the love of God in their lives and live it out, often totally oblivious to the fact that they are doing so.

This comes out of the loss of self into the mystery of God. We see it in Gerard Manley Hopkins' poem *That Nature is a Heraclitan Fire and of the Comfort of the Resurrection* when he writes:

> I am all at once what Christ is, since he was what I am, and
> This Jack, joke, poor potsherd, 'patch, matchwood,
>   immortal diamond,
> Is immortal diamond.

We see it in one of Berthold Brecht's final poems when he writes:

> Already for some time
> I had lost all fear of death.
> For nothing
> Can be wrong with me if I myself
> Am nothing.[75]

Here is a resurrection faith that looks to a new dawn, knowing that God brings it, wills it and that His vast treasury of faith is available new every morning to the whole of humanity. At the heart of faith is the realisation that every morning is a new day. That when we fall we can be picked up and we can start again. W.H. Vanstone expressed it as well as anyone in his poem *Morning Glory, Starlit Sky* which we will now sing.

---

75. B. Brecht, *Poems*, p. 451 - 52

The Worcester Pieta – an interpretation
Worcester Cathedral
July 1991

Deuteronomy 33: v. 27:
The eternal God is your refuge, and underneath are the everlasting arms

In the year 1498, Jacopo Galli Rome drew up a contract for the twenty-three year old Michaelangelo in which he agreed:

> At his own proper cost (to) make a Pieta; that is to say, a draped figure of the Virgin Mary with the dead Christ in her arms, the figures being life size, for the sum of four hundred and fifty gold ducats in papal gold, to be finished within the term of one year from the beginning of the work.

The contract goes on to state that the Pieta shall be:

> More beautiful than any work in marble to be seen in Rome today, and such that no master of our own time shall be able to produce a better.

The Pieta was a form of sculpture developed about a century before in Germany as a special expression of Christian devotion. It has no Scriptural origin. The nearest we get is the description of the deposition of Our Lord from the Cross in the Passion narratives. The Gospel writers tell us that Mary was at the foot of the Cross so that it does not take much imagination to see her holding the body of her dead son. The word Pieta simply means 'pity'; it is an expression of the pain and agony of motherhood, echoing the words of Simeon in the Temple that 'you too will be pierced to the heart.'

In Italian art, Mary is usually depicted with St. John, thus following the example of St. John's Gospel. In the Michelangelo Pieta Mary is seated on a rocky ledge, with her knees apart, the leg which supports the upper part of Christ's body being slightly higher. Her head is bowed. One arm encircles the shoulders of the Christ supporting his head. Her right hand holds his body against her own. Her left hand with upturned palm signifies passive acceptance. Her flowing robe surrounds the body giving support for the very limp body. His depiction of Mary's acceptance of the death of her son is in strong contrast to the depiction of some of his contemporaries who show her full of agony and grief.

His depiction of the dead Christ is of a lifeless figure. The head

93

falls back against Mary's arm. The right arm hangs completely limp. The body is that of a young man. All the joints of the body are delineated to emphasise the potentiality for movement and action. The wounds of Christ are minimised. The piercing of the nails and the spear are small. There is no overemphasis here in the pain and suffering of Christ as in the Grunewald Altarpiece. This depicts a very diseased and wounded Christ reflecting the time when society was itself suffering the pains of the Black Death. Rather Michelangelo is emphasising the physical perfection of He who reveals the Godhead.

Towards the end of his life, when he was 92, Michelangelo returned to the theme of the Pieta for the last time. The Rondanini Pieta, as it is called, is a very different work. He was dying as he carved it and it remained unfinished. Gone are all the polished surfaces and the fine perfection. This piece has very rough surfaces. It contains, as one writer has put it

> Strange dissonances and disproportions, facial figures which are only vaguely suggested, an unexplained disjunction of the arm at the side of Christ's body and finally, the quivering un-terminated arc of the two fragile bodies.[76]

It seems very likely that after he had roughed out the piece he made considerable changes and did not live long enough to complete the changes. So Christ has a third arm which has not been removed while the new right arm has only been roughed out and hangs diagonally along his body next to Mary. The figures are almost standing and their faces are close together. Mary just higher than the sagging Christ figure. The sculpture still speaks of acceptance rather than agony, but the body of the son is pressed against the frail frame of his mother. Individual identity seems to be lost in a deep symbol of self-offering and suffering. Some see this Pieta of marking the agonised expression of the greatness and the limitation of classicism in Christian art. It can also be seen as looking in a new direction and offers a new way in Christian art which is seen more clearly in El Greco and the twentieth century expressionists.

Worcester Cathedral now has its own Pieta. It has been donated by the Friends of the Cathedral in order to mark the contribution of eighty artists to the Cathedral Appeal. Glyn Williams, the sculptor, is one of the leading exponents of this art in the country today. When the Cathedral Fabric Commission was asked if we might have this piece in

---

76. Source unknown

the Cathedral, they were delighted. It is a very fine work of art, but many will wish to have an interpretation of it. I have talked to Glyn Williams who sees this piece very much as an expression of suffering humanity. He is also very clear that his inspiration is the Rondanini Pieta. We see this in the deliberately rough carving, in the emphasis on the arms. He points to the way that the Rondanini Pieta has little emphasis on weight and that the two figures seem to rise up together without almost any physical contact. It is, he says, an aspiring sculpture of a young child, very limp and dead, with the head unsupported. The right hand hangs lifeless in an identical position to that in the Michelangelo Pieta. But look at the very strong hands and arms which support the body. They express power and assurance, they are in some way the hands of more than a mother, they are like the hands of one who supports the whole world. Glyn Williams has deliberately removed any reference to gender. The emphasis is on the carrying strength of the arms. The child is all children, identifiable to the viewer in any way they wish. The stone is deliberately rough, matching the Rondinini. Glyn Williams wanted to remove sentimentality. There is here plenty of emotion but not any nostalgia for other expressions of the same subject.

The tone of the Pieta sits well in the Crypt. It looks as if it has always been there. The helpless figure does indeed express suffering humanity. I see in it the victims of the Holocaust, Hiroshima, the starving and suffering of today's world, the exploitation of children and the pain of war. The figure expresses the helplessness of all who are victims of this world's violence. It affirms that the suffering Christ is suffering in all these people. There is here, all the pain and agony of humanity and the sense of helplessness which we all feel when faced with such pain. But there is more than that. These powerful arms affirm first of all the strength of motherhood, something not often recognised. It says more than 'Underneath are the everlasting arms.'

The God of Deuteronomy is one who cares for and carries his people, like a father or mother would carry a distressed child. Faced with pain, agony and helplessness, we can be assured not only that God is in the pain but also that he carries us through it. The figure may be that of a dead child, but I was reminded that death is something we all face. We all become helpless and childlike. Sitting looking at the Sculpture, I was drawn to that passage in the end of St John's Gospel where the risen Christ says to Peter,

When you were young, you fastened your belt about you and walked where you chose; but when you are old, you will stretch out your arms and a stranger will bind you fast, and carry you where you have no wish to go (John 21: v. 18)

For, at the end of the day, we shall all be carried where we would not go, but still we are assured that the helpless and powerless God is still with us. The Pieta is not a distinctively Anglican symbol – it is much more Catholic and Continental - but I am pleased and proud to have this work in the Cathedral for several reasons:

- We are grateful to the artists who helped us raise money for the restoration.
- We are proud to carry on the tradition of promoting and encouraging the arts of all sorts. Only so will Art survive.
- We have a piece which not only blends in well, but is also a real encouragement to devotion.
- We are enabled to recall the terrible suffering and violence during this century.
- But above all, we can, through the Pieta, celebrate the triumph of Jesus in and through suffering and that God is ever with us for *'underneath are the everlasting arms.'*

Michelangelo expressed something of what he was after in a sonnet which itself helps us to understand both his work and the Worcester Pieta:

Through many years and many trials searched
The right conception of a living form
To the wise man will come
In tough hard stone, when he is soon to die.
For only late we reach
Strange and exalted things, and do not stay.

The Future of Cathedrals:
Reflections following a world tour of Anglican cathedrals
2000

A major new phenomenon of the last few years is the building of new large Cathedrals in post-communist Eastern Europe. Some of them are vast and reflect a real commitment of money, some of it from dubious sources. It does not take much to see what they are about. They are not about the need of Bishops for new cathedrals. They are about the development and preservation of a new nationalism and using the church in the old familiar way to consecrate and bolster up the status quo. A recent article described the opening of the Cathedral of Christ the Saviour in Moscow in August 2001. It cost over US$500million. 16,000 people attended the consecration. The idea of the building was the project of the Mayor of Moscow but it was not without controversy. One critic put it like this: 'The rebuilding of the Christ the Saviour Cathedral and the inevitable political and financial scandals that will arise will once and for all alienate the nations from the Church and from Orthodoxy.' The church leaders took the reverse view seeing it as 'the restoration of Orthodoxy to the centre of Russian life' (Ecumenical News Bulletin).

In Poland, the foundation stone of a 27,000-ft basilica, costing US$ 45million was blessed by Pope John Paul in 1999. But last December, Cardinal Glemp stopped the building on the grounds that the expense involved was 'inappropriate for a place of worship'. A further comment was made by the chairman of the committee that recommended the suspension of the project:

'It is clear this project must be rethought entirely or exchanged for another. Churches aren't the same as commercial office blocks, which pay for themselves and are often renovated. They're intended to last for centuries, not just 40-50 years.' It was estimated that the sheet glass used in the basilica's giant canopy would need replacing every four years.

We do not tend to think of the English Cathedrals in the same way. After all, every English Diocese has a cathedral and some are much grander than others. They are where the Bishop has his seat. The Care of Cathedrals Measure of 1989 and the new 1999 Cathedrals Measure (at the insistence of the Deans) describes cathedrals as 'Centres of worship and mission.'

Is that what they are? Is that how they work and was that why they were built? The great early English Cathedrals and some Abbeys were built or rebuilt by the Normans with castles nearby as a way of suppressing and civilising the natives. So they too were a focus of a new nationalism. They had a political dimension. Admittedly there were some like St Wulfstan of Worcester who not only survived the Norman Conquest but also subverted some of the Norman influence. But even he rebuilt his Cathedral in a grand Norman style. There is no time to give a brief history of Cathedrals; but Cathedrals, as we now know them, are very much the fruit of Victorian reflection on the role and place of Cathedrals.

The 19th century was a nasty shock to Cathedrals. In 1844 they were asset-stripped to help to find resources to enable the Church to respond to the needs of new urban areas emerging out of the Industrial Revolution. This was followed by the creation of new Dioceses in the Church of England, which raised questions about the need and role of Cathedrals. The Tractarians argued for Cathedrals as centres of Diocesan life and as a resource to the diocese. (Hence the development of theological colleges in cathedral closes). There was also a massive restoration of cathedrals during the 19th century, putting lots of money into the pockets of Gilbert Scott (as well as Stanford, Stainer, Gore, Ouseley etc.) and a resurgence of Cathedral music.

To jump a bit: the period since the Second World War created a new debate centring initially on the rebuilding of Coventry Cathedral and the completion of various other cathedrals like Liverpool and Guildford. The two World Wars had also focused cathedrals as centres of national identity and as place to establish war memorials, etc. In 1966 the Revd. Albert van den Heuval, then youth secretary of the World Council of Churches delivered a paper to the Deans and Provosts of England at Coventry on the function for the Cathedral in the community today. This was a seminal paper[77] and I discovered on my visit in the year 2000 to Cathedrals around the world that it has reverberated around the Cathedral world. He begins by asserting quite rightly that:

Cathedrals can never be essential to the Christian faith. Essential to the Christian faith is the faithfulness of God. Cathedrals may be good tools, they may be bad tools, they can be corrupted, they can be relevant; but in themselves they are neutral.

This statement is a very accurate account of what Cathedrals have been throughout the history of the Church. He then offers fourteen images of what a Cathedral might be and do, and while what he offers

77. Van den Heuval, A.E. (1966): 'The functions of a cathedral in the community today 'in *Papers read at a Conference of Deans and Provosts in Britain*, held at Coventry Cathedral 22 – 25 April 1966, under the chairmanship of the Rev. Roger Lloyd.: Coventry Cathedral/Church of England

has been reflected on, rarely has it been fully worked out anywhere. All I can do here is list them:

A sign of pro-existence - Cathedrals to serve the structures of the world.
A symbol of diversity in unity - Cathedrals to reflect the pluralism and plurality of society.
A Pentecostal laboratory - Cathedrals teaching people to integrate the poetic, the music, the artistic and the dramatic into the Gospel and into life.
The Theatre of Basic Drama - Cathedrals where in liturgy and drama the fundamental truths of life are communicated
A Temple of Dialogue - Cathedrals where people learn to have real conversation (and listening) across the barriers of society.
A Centre of Creativity - Cathedrals where people can discern to separate valuable things from things not worth knowing.
An Academy of Committed Information - Cathedrals where people are helped to deal with real information and not propaganda.
A Clinic for Public Exorcism - Which will enable people to unmask the demons of society.
An International Exchange - Cathedrals as centres where people of many lands and cultures encounter each other.
A Broadcasting Station for the Voices of the Poor - Cathedrals as centres which speak for the oppressed and those who have no one to speak for them.
A Tower of Reconciliation - Cathedrals to encourage reconciliation but without avoiding the suffering involved.
A Motel for Pilgrims - Cathedrals as providing facilities for people on a journey.
A House of the Vicarious Feasts - Cathedrals as places for feasts, parties and celebrations.
A Hut of the Shepherd - Cathedrals as centres for the Bishop's Pastoral work.

In the 1970s and 1980s a vast range of Cathedral Appeals developed. The Victorian Restorations needed restoring. Since 1990, following pressure from the conservation lobby, Cathedrals required to have Fabric Advisory Committees - all answerable to the Cathedrals' Fabric Commission. It was a *quid pro quo* for taking English Heritage money for work on Cathedrals.

Since the 1970s, Britain moved into tourism mode and Cathedrals went along with that. When I became a Dean in 1987, the great slogan was that Cathedrals were there "to turn tourists into pilgrims." One of my great fears is that, not least through the granting of Heritage and Lottery money, Cathedrals have been caught up in the Heritage business with its audio-visual presentations, visitors' centres, shops, cafés etc. This becomes self-perpetuating because of the need to raise money for Cathedrals. A recent survey has shown a noticeable drop in visitors to all Cathedrals over the last three years. The use of tourism as a money-spinner is coming to an end. It was yet another culture trap. At the same time attendance at worship in Cathedrals has been growing significantly.

In the 1980s the Cathedrals were getting a bad press through events like the saga at Lincoln Cathedral[78], the Mappa Mundi affair at Hereford[79] and various other rather less publicised events. The Howe Commission was set up, at the request of the Association of English Cathedrals, to look into the problems and opportunities facing Cathedrals. The report, which was entitled *Heritage and Renewal* (1994) gave a clear overview of the state of Cathedral life. Every Cathedral was visited by members of the Commission and a total review of the financial state was also included. New legislation ensued. There was a financial reform whereby all Cathedral accounts now have a common format. The new *Cathedrals Measure* makes some radical changes. Chapters had to be enlarged to include lay people with proper expertise. There is considerable flexibility in rewriting the statutes and a new Cathedral council has to be set up to which the Dean and Chapter are to report at least twice a year. The Dean is given new powers as a sort of Chief Executive Officer. All this legislation came on the top of the *Care of Cathedrals Measure* 1990.

It is already beginning to be seen, even before every Cathedral has implemented the Measure that the legislation was to some extent, an over-reaction. While these new bodies are being put in place, nothing is removed. The whole matter of how communication takes place in an increasingly complex structure is not clear.

---

78. See, for example, media coverage here: http://www.nytimes.com/1996/01/24/ world/lincoln-journal-cathedral-schism-causing-high-church-dudgeon.html (accessed 28.05.17)
79. In 1988, the Dean and Chapter of Hereford Cathedral proposed selling the priceless *Mappa Mundi* due to a funding crisis. A huge outcry ensued.

Can the Anglican Communion Hang Together?

A Paper to 'Affirming Catholicism', Oxford

13th November, 2000

First of all, I need to give you a little bit of autobiography so that you can see where I am coming from. As long ago as 1964, I went to work at Church House Westminster as Study Secretary of the Missionary & Ecumenical Council of the Church Assembly. Just after I started work I was sent on a tour of the Church in West Africa. These were heady days for the Anglican Communion. The old British Empire and Commonwealth was breaking up. New nations were rapidly emerging. The Anglican Communion was drastically changing. It was Archbishop Fisher who convened both the 1948 and 1958 Lambeth Conferences who had encouraged the development of Provinces in the Anglican Communion and his became vital with the growth of independent nations. The conference in Toronto in 1964 called for 'Mutual Interdependence and Responsibility in the Body of Christ'. This was a way of trying to get a proper sharing among Anglicans and levels of mutual support in the provinces. Paternalism was on the way out. But ecumenism was also riding high. Union schemes between Anglican and other non-Roman Churches were under active consideration in almost every Province of the Anglican Communion. We had a vision of the Anglican Communion gradually vanishing into national United Churches. Moreover, the Second Vatican Council was meeting and the dramatic changes taking place there were full of hope.

I was on the staff of the 1968 Lambeth Conference. This too was seen as a major turning point but it was not that well prepared. The post of the Anglican Executive Officer had been in place for some time, and following the Conference there was to be established the Anglican Consultative Council. This, in the future, was to be the main decision making body for the Anglican Communion. It was to consist of Bishops, clergy and laity and many saw it as replacing the Lambeth Conference. Bill Jacob in his excellent *The Making of the Anglican Church world-wide* (1997) points out that the Lambeth Conference was a very English operation; the majority of the bishops at 1958 Lambeth Conference were English. The Americans were suspicious of this. There were only three African Bishops present, and five Indians. There was not much enthusiasm to continue the Lambeth Conference at that time and people spoke of Anglicanism something wanting to die to achieve a wider unity.

From 1968 onwards, I have sat on the edge of the debates and shared in parts of them. In the 1980s, following the 1978 Lambeth Conference (the calling of which had been strongly opposed from USA and Canada but demanded by the great number of African and Asian Bishops) the Communion entered into the exercise of 'Partners In Mission' (PIM) whereby conferences were held in every Province which was attended by partners from other parts of the Anglican communion in order to assess priorities in mission. It is not clear that it succeeded, and it cost a lot of money. The PIM exercise in England led to a criticism by Africans of the lack of Evangelism. I attended the PIM exercise in Scotland. I also attended the ACC meeting in the Panama in 1996 and just this last year I have been on a tour of USA, New Zealand, Australia and South Africa. The point of this visit was to look at the organisation and administration of Cathedrals in the Anglican Communion. So at this point I would like to be slightly anecdotal about this trip of mine, and then try and relate that to the subject of this paper.

I could regale you at some length with stories from my trip and indeed may slip in a few. But what I would really like to do is to draw on some of the work I have done to think little about these provinces.

USA

The key to understanding the Episcopal Church in the USA is that it is a profoundly Congregational church. All the power lies in the congregation. To give you an extreme example of this, the Diocese of Fort Worth was created in 1984 and a large suburban Church designated as the Cathedral. After 18 months the congregation asked the bishop to take his chair away they were finding it too expensive to be a Cathedral. So he did. The extreme Congregationalism, whereby even Deans of Cathedrals are appointed by the Congregational search committee give the laity a strong role. It also poses deep questions about the role of the Bishop. Thus Bishops tend to be rather autocratic and there are a large number of them. Except for a few very large dioceses, Bishops often have about 30 or 40 clergy in their Diocese, even though the Dioceses often cover vast areas. The role of the bishop in the House of bishops is also very different to England because all the retired Bishops remain members. At the same time the churches have a stronger social role than England because the whole society depends on all the churches for the relief of the poor and the homeless. Similarly, the Church-State divide means that the churches provide a strong basis for Christian education.

The Episcopal Church is a minority Church but a very elite one. There was a deliberate strategy in attracting the rich and the powerful into Episcopalianism through the provision of private education. But it also gives the Church a significant political profile. Dean Sayer of Washington was not only the grandson of President Woodrow Wilson (and born in the White House) but also a strong campaigner for Civil Rights and opposed to the Vietnam War. This social elitism is on the wane but there are growing number of Hispanic congregations in ECUSA which may well shift the social basis of the Church in years to come.

America is also a place of extremes, shifting from Bishop Spong at one end, to extreme fundamentalist Churches at the other. Clergy discipline seems to be much more lax than in England. There is also a very profound search for real spirituality among many people and this is reflected in one or two very thriving Religious Communities.

The General Convention in the USA last summer proved to be a place of compromise when people were fearing the opposite. But there is a big debate over the role of gay priests. The opponents of the ordination of women are a small minority and there are growing number of women Bishops. The ECUSA Prayer Book of 1970 has served extremely well and there seems to be little desire for revision.

New Zealand

The Church in New Zealand seems to me to be more integrated. One diocese (Nelson) is dominated by extreme charismatic congregations with the result that the only Church with liturgical worship is the Cathedral. But Anglicanism is pretty dominant in that country. Among the small population of 3.5million, Anglicans are 33% of the population. The figure of Bishop George Augustus Selwyn still looms over everything but it does not seem to be a church full of tensions. There is an enormous respect for the Maori culture and considerable integration with the use of a creative new Prayer Book.

Australia

Australia is much more worrying. In spite of a firm stand by Archbishop Goodhew, it looks as if the very rich Diocese of Sydney is moving more and more into an extreme evangelical position. The brothers Jenson, one of who heads Moore Theological College, the other runs a highly successful Church seem destined to take over. Many ordinands in Sydney Diocese would attend Baptist churches in any other part of Australia. The election of the new primate proved to be very divisive and the election of Archbishop Carnley, who is a well known academic and radical theologian, seems set to push Sydney into a more extreme position. Australia tends to be dominated by its provincial structures but there are now threats of church planting from the Diocese of Sydney elsewhere, which many find very distasteful. There is a huge national agenda in relation to aboriginal people and a growing group of Aboriginal theologians.

South Africa

The Church of the Province of South Africa is in a very delicate state. The great battle to oppose apartheid held the church together under the leadership of Desmond Tutu. But now the battle is won, the Church seems to be not quite clear what it is for. There is pressure towards indigenisation, which is regarded with some suspicion in some places. The Archbishop is campaigning hard for the abolition of Third World debt but a country with a terrible AIDS epidemic and 60% unemployment faces massive problems and the social structure is very frail. The CPSA is a far more liberal church than other provinces in Africa. Having campaigned hard for the ending of apartheid and ordained women early on, it takes quite a liberal stance on the issue of homosexuality, a stance which is rejected in most other parts of Africa.

If we look wider in the Anglican Communion, we see whole dioceses in Canada facing abolition because of the cost of meeting child abuse cases. We see pressures both ways over the Act of Synod following the Ordination of Women in England. We see provinces failing to make their proper contribution to the work of the ACC and those failures headed up by USA, Canada, Australia and England. This raises several questions. It could be a sign of a lack of commitment to the Anglican Communion or it could be lack of trust in the present structures, which is a different matter. It might represent (and this is most likely) a turning in and a ghettoisation of the provinces looking in on themselves instead of out to the world. That certainly is what is happening in England. The review of structures set up by the Turnbull Commission provides some welcome rationalisation of financial arrangements but the imposition of the Archbishop's Council has tightened the centre very greatly. When you tighten the centre everything spins away from it. The central structures are in danger of becoming irrelevant to the life of Dioceses and parishes. Moreover as more money comes from the parishes the CofE becomes increasingly Congregational. It is a very noticeable both in relation to both the Church of England and the Anglican Communion that every reorganisation or restructuring adds to the levels of administration. There is an unwillingness to streamline and abolish some bits and it leads to structural inertia.

It used to be said that the things which held the Anglican Communion together were:

a. The Lambeth Quadrilateral used as a basis of what Anglicans believed and for dialogue over matters of unity. This consists of:
- Common submission to Scripture as the Word of God, the uniquely authoritative record of God's revelation of himself to humanity
- Common profession of the faith derived from that revelation especially witnessed to in the primitive creeds
- Common acceptance of the divinely instituted sacraments of Baptism and Holy Communion
- Common acknowledgement of a ministry through which the grace of God is given to his people

In many ways, this has now been superseded by the Ecumenical agreements on Baptism, Eucharist and Ministry.

b. The centrality of Scripture, Tradition and Reason as the basis of faith.
c. A Common Prayer Book and liturgy
d. Communion with the See of Canterbury

But as Bill Jacob pointed out: 'an awful lot had been taken for granted. The embodiment of Anglicanism is still largely Anglo-Saxon, despite national expressions of faith, order and worship of the Catholic Church. Many expatriates had departed. English church structures and titles and robes and vestments are customarily adopted. Much more important for the Communion than issues like the ordination of women is the embodiment of the Christian faith in cultures other than western European. Indigenous theologies, spiritualities and worship are needed. An incarnational faith must require that people that engage with that faith work it into their own contexts' (pp. 298 – 9).

We have to remember that the first Lambeth Conference was called at the instigation of Archbishop Grey of Cape Town because of the actions of Bishop Colenso in Natal. Colenso was ahead of his time. He was a keen proponent of Biblical Criticism and a great supporter of indigenisation. He wanted to open the church to polygamous believers. So there is a sense in which the things which threaten the communion today can be seen in the Colenso affair. Indigenisation, Biblical interpretation and sex. It is notable that those busy condemning homosexuality have not been equally vocal on the subject of polygamy which has been a matter of concern for most Lambeth Conferences and a matter where the Provinces have operating differing disciplines.

What is pulling the Anglican Communion apart? Those things which used to hold it together no longer have the same force. The ACC has not fulfilled people's expectations of it. Moreover, the role of the Archbishop of Canterbury has been boosted both by the continuing of the Lambeth Conference and by the development of the Primate's meeting which he also chairs. Dialogue with Rome and the ARCIC[80] report *The Gift of Authority* (1998) raise a spectre of the Archbishop becoming a sort of Anglican Patriarch, but it is not the only way things could go. It is important to remember that as far back as the 1878 Lambeth Conference, the following agreements were established:

1. The duly verified action of every self-governing church in the exercise of its own discipline should be respected by all other churches and their individual members.
2. No bishop or other minister from one self-governing church should in any sense exercise his ministry in a diocese in any other self-governing church without the permission of the bishop of that diocese.
3. No bishop should allow a minister coming from another self-governing church to exercise his ministry in his diocese unless the minister brought with him letters and testimonials from his previous bishop.
4. No self-governing church should consecrate a bishop as a missionary bishop in any place to which a bishop had already been sent by some other church of the Communion.

In other words, it is the level of mutual respect which is central. Thus when Bishop R.O. Hall ordained a woman in Hong Kong in 1944 and Bishop Gilbert Baker his successor did the same later, the matter of respect for the autonomy of provinces was a key to holding the Communion together. In a way something similar is revealed in the Act of Synod.

---

80. Anglican Roman Catholic International Commission (http://www. anglicancommunion.org/ relationships/ecumenical-dialogues/roman-catholic/arcic.aspx)

Where then are the points of division?

Liturgy

Lambeth 1958 laid down principles for prayer book revision in the light of liturgical scholarship. This has now moved forward and everyone is more into the principles for a flexible liturgy. This is very difficult to use as the base of coherence. For instance, there has been a strong Maori input into the NZ prayer book.

Indigenisation

A lack of sense of a need to relate to indigenous culture is just beginning to move. My discussions with clergy from the diocese of Kimberley revealed a very confused picture as to what is essential and what is divisive. The desire to incorporate some old tribal customs into the Christian faith and worship seems to be coming through. Yet alongside this, the churches do not relate to the African Independent Churches, which arose as a protest against a church dominated by western culture. The process has been more successful in India but it is a long slow process.

New Zealand also revealed another aspect of this in the person of the Dean of Christ Church, who, as ex director of Communications at the WCC has a strong sense of the need to engage with the culture. He has devised flexible liturgies and a service for people who don't go to Church. As liturgy becomes more a tool to use than a set text to follow, there will be many diverse expressions of worship emerging.

The Charismatic Movement

We have already seen more flexible liturgy through the Charismatic Movement. In South Africa, many white people retreated into the Charismatic Movement in order to avoid the challenge of apartheid and it was never very popular with the black clergy. They disliked its intolerance. In its more intolerant forms Charismatic congregations reject those who differ from them and enforce a new sort of conformity. It is also becoming clear that it is a major factor in people leaving the Church. It lacks spiritual depth and the intellectual rigour which mature people need to sustain their faith.

Homosexuality

The Lambeth Conference in 1998 fell apart over this issue and it has become a very divisive matter in a way that people outside the

Church fail to understand. Bishop Michael Doe in his recent book *Seeking the Truth in Love* (2000) shows how this matter is being tackled and it is a sign of hope that the General Convention in the USA managed to hold together. The bitter divisions over homosexuality in USA and around the world have hermeneutics at the base. Much depends on how scripture is interpreted. Homophobia is a deep issue which requires a great deal of pastoral concern and sensitivity, as does racism. Michael Doe calls for the same thing as Lambeth 1878. The Communion needs to live with difference and diversity but also show a level of pastoral care and concern which was not clear at Lambeth. Attached to this issue are matters of cultural shift and how society understands itself. Equally important and still unresolved and yet has not been so divisive is the lack of agreement about how to treat polygamy. It was at the 1958 conference where a Nigerian bishop attacked the Western Church for condemning the open polygamy of African society while doing little about the successive polygamy of Western society.

Tribalism
    The way in which there has been a proliferation of dioceses in Kenya and other parts of Africa reflects tribalism to a great extent. This means that each tribe wants its own bishop. This can be a denial of catholicity. The terrible situation in Rwanda has deep tribal origins and some very bad behaviour by some church leaders. Unfortunately, the Anglican Communion lacks the legal structure to regulate matters of this sort when they go really wrong. And these matters, we need to note, have taken place in a situation of Church growth. But tribalism is not just an African problem. Bishop Peter Selby pointed out several years ago in his book *Belonging* (1991) that the sense of true belonging in the church, which some might call catholicity, rejects the tribal. This is expressed in the Church of England over race, sex and leadership at the present time. We are full of interest groups trying to preserve their own identity just like a tribe. So the church in the west has little reason to pass judgement on others.

The emergence of a multi-faith world
    In the USA I found many Cathedrals using the phase that they were 'Centres of prayer of all people' to make them centres for interfaith dialogue and indeed interfaith worship. The phrase was originally used in the early days of the ecumenical movement to encourage Cathedrals to be symbols of Christian unity by greeting people of other denominations

and some constitutions made provisions for non-Anglican Canons on Cathedral chapters. But many will find the multi faith aspect threatening and will be seen again as showing a dangerously liberal trend. I suspect that this will become a really major issue, which could divide Anglicans during the next 100 years.

Thus we face great dangers from those seeking to pursue a pure and clear faith. From those who wish to plant their own version of the faith in other Dioceses, from those who wish to impose one view on any particular issue on others whose whole cultural base and context is totally different. Can the Anglican Communion hang together? Only if it resists these trends. Only if it affirms diversity and respects boundaries. Maybe we need to recapture the view of Anglicanism as a temporary phenomenon preparing the way for the Coming Great Church. Once we absolutise Anglicanism, we make it turn in on itself and thereby tear itself in pieces.

Can Anglicanism hang together? Only if every part of it becomes a lot more tolerant, affirming and respecting differences and allowing space for a variety of expressions of the faith. If it does not do this, then it does not deserve to survive, because it will have ceased to be Anglican anyhow.

Revisiting 'The Imitation'
2013

Dr Samuel Johnson said of *The Imitation of Christ* "It must be a good book as the whole world has opened its arms to it." What is it about the book that has made to it so attractive over nearly five centuries? Allowing for its 15th Century assumptions, it has a deep understanding of human nature and what it means to be a Christian. It reveals a faith, which has a deep sense of devotion and priorities for living. It understands the costliness of faith and inspires those with a pioneering spirit, who do not take easily to institutional religion. It is a good read for today.

The book was originally four separate books and completed by 1427. It has never been out of print since its first printing at Augsburg in 1471. Its author, Thomas a Kempis (1379-1471) an Augustinian monk was a member of a movement in the Low Countries known as The Modern Devotion (*Devotio Moderna*) which called mainly lay people into serious discipleship. Soon after it was written, it was circulated in England by the Carthusians. The English translation made by Richard Whytford (1478-1542) became very popular and by 1860 had been through 446 editions. There have been many other English translations as well as into other languages, including Hebrew.

The influence of the book over the centuries has been vast. Luther, Calvin and Ignatius Loyola, founder of the Jesuits, all came under its influence. We see its influence in many Jesuit writers like Gerard Manley Hopkins and Teilhard de Chardin. In the seventeenth century, Jeremy Taylor wrote his own version called *The Great Exemplar*, William Laud was another devotee, and we find John Wesley deeply influenced by it. He required every Methodist home to have copy. He gave his version the title The Christian Pattern and issued guidelines on how to use it.

It was popular among Evangelicals and Catholics and some translators gave the text various slants to suit their own presuppositions. The evangelical preacher John Newton was converted when he came across a copy. Many great Victorian figures read it including General Gordon and William Gladstone. It became a frequent confirmation gift, though the pseudo-Jacobean language of some translations was not helpful. George Eliot wrote powerfully about it in *The Mill on the Floss.*

Among the Tractarians we find it being read aloud in Religious Communities, as well as by individuals. In 1890, Dr Liddon published a translation in blank verse. St Theresa of Liseaux described it as "Dear Imitation...nothing would part me from my little book" and Pope John

XXIII read it every year in retreat. In India, Ghandi valued it and the Hindu philosopher Swami Vivekananda (1863-1902) translated chapters into Bengali. Three great Irish writers, Oscar Wilde, Samuel Beckett and James Joyce acknowledged its influence. Billy Graham encouraged his converts to read it.

Dietrich Bonhoeffer's *The Cost of Discipleship* is his version. He left his own Latin edition to Bishop Bell and in a letter commented 'In the *Imitation of Christ* I read "Take good care of your cell and it will take good care of you."' Dag Hammarskjold copied quotations into his book, *Markings*. The latest reference I have found is in *The Life of Pi*.

It is sixty years since Penguin Classics published its last edition. I was deeply honoured to provide what I hope is a 21st century text, which is faithful to the original. This book has done more than any other book to encourage Christians to be faithful and that was its original intention.

The Imitation of Christ by Thomas a Kempis: translated by Robert Jeffery, with an introduction by Max von Habsburg, is published by Penguin Classics.

Uxbridge Road

St Mary's Barnes

Advent Sunday, 2001

Isaiah 2: v. 3:
All nations shall stream towards it and many people will go and say "Let us go to the mountain of the Lord"
Matthew 24: v. 44:
The Son of Man will come at a time when you least expect him

Whenever I travel from Oxford to London, I usually come on the bus service known as the Oxford Tube, which has the advantage of running every 12 minutes and being very cheap. It means that we come into London on the M40 and A40, which used to be known as the Western Avenue. That great Anglican spiritual writer Evelyn Underhill has a poem about that road which is now even more appropriate than when she originally wrote it and in it she is making a point about how we encounter God in our daily lives. It is too long to read all of it but here is the first verse:

The Western Road goes streaming out to seek the cleanly wild,
It pours the city's dim desires towards the undefiled,
It sweeps betwixt the huddled homes about its eddies grown
To smear the little space between the city and the sown:
The torments of that seething tide who is there that can see?
There's one who walked with starry feet the western road by me.

Not only does this poem affirm God in the ordinary things of life, but it also expresses the sense of movement which lies at the heart of God. It is that sense of movement which can be seen in both readings. The people of God coming to the mountain of God and the Son of man coming to humanity at a time we do not expect. There is nothing static about the biblical view of God. He is sending God, who sends his son. The parable of the wise and foolish Virgins sums it up in the phrase Behold the Bridegroom cometh, Go ye out to meet him. As we move towards God, we find he has moved towards us. In the everyday affairs of life there is God with us and goes before us. Today's Gospel puts it all in the contact of daily living, marrying, dancing, drinking, eating and working. There, right there, is God.

The Advent season reflects that sense of movement, as it looks forward to the coming together of all things in Christ. It is not really

112

clear what this means. Many suspect that the early Church got it wrong. In the trial of Jesus in response to the question - "Are you Christ?", Jesus replies quoting the Book of Daniel, "I am, and you will see the Son of Man coming in the clouds of glory". But in Daniel that coming is the coming of God in heaven not a coming again on the earth. But it is for as we experience "the one who walked with starry feet along the western road" we ever experience God in the present moment, in the here and now and that is, in a sense, an ever present coming of Christ.

It was forty years ago in October that I came to this parish to serve a second curacy with Chris Heath. He was the man who had nurtured my vocation at St. Paul's and he gave me space to try things out. Next June, I shall retire after forty-three years of ministry. There was a profound contrast between the two curacies. I moved from depressed poverty-ridden shipbuilding and mining Sunderland to the comparatively affluent articulate influential Barnes. I learned a vast amount and made many friends in both parishes. Since then I have had a rather unusual ecclesiastical career ending up as a Canon at the strangest Cathedral in the Anglican Communion.

My family life has been fulfilling but changed six years ago with the sudden death of my wife. Through it all I have learned more about myself, and more about this strange, ever moving, demanding, loving, ultimately unapproachable God who ever goes before us and never lets us rest. This is not a comfortable God, but a disturbing God ever calling us out of ourselves, ever wanting us to take up his cross and follow him. It is now clear from the writings of the social historian Callum Brown in his book *The Death of Christian Britain* that I and my contemporaries were part of a religious revival. This hit Britain between 1945 and 1963 and faded out altogether to be replaced by an increasingly secular society.

All this has led me to remain unrepentantly radical and liberal. It has led me to be more and more impatient with a Church, which, faced as it has been in this very secular age, of opting either for the ghetto or the wilderness chose the ghetto. It has turned in on itself and ever seeks a pattern of self-preservation at a time when, above all, it needs to take risks, to listen, reach out and forget itself in God. So I remain convinced of the centrality of God as revealed in Jesus Christ and less and less interested in the Church as an institution.

I recall many events from my time at Barnes, but two stick with me:

1. Pope John XXIII died and we all went to a requiem mass in the Catholic Church. Pope John had opened the windows of the Vatican and breathed a new spirit into the Church, but now, nearly all the windows and doors had been shut again.

2. In 1963 the Bishop of Woolwich, John Robinson, published *Honest to God*. It was a moment of dialogue and evangelism. Night after night, week after week, I found myself in people's houses until the early hours of the morning talking theology with people saying "Thank God a Bishop has said what we really think". It was a creative turning point when new life could have flooded into the Church, and for many it did. But when that even greater and more profound prophet Bishop David Jenkins raised even deeper issues, he was denounced, misquoted and rebutted by a fearful church. Honest intellectual enquiry can never be wrong. God is never limited by our definitions of him. He comes to disturb, to challenge, to open wide our minds and hearts.

But I am not pessimistic - rather the reverse.

Last year I made a tour of the Anglican Communion, visiting America, New Zealand, Australia and South Africa and here and there, in strange places and in odd corners, I was aware that the one with starry feet is moving, stirring up new life, new spirituality and new hope. It was well expressed for me in the writings of David Tacey, an Australian professor of literature, in a book entitled *Re-Enchantment* (2000). He is discovering a new spirituality which arises from below and within. It is a discovery of the sacred in the ordinary and in sensitivity to others, which reaches out in all directions. It is a faith which accepts no boundaries and which takes risks and finds new ways. He quotes Cardinal Martini of Milan as calling for Christians to renounce their conventional faith and to discover a faith which wells up from the mystery of our being and from the ground of our unknowing. Tacey argues, and this is matched by my own experience, that Christianity is always reaching out towards a deeper purpose but never gets there. He writes: 'We lose confidence in the grace and fluidity of the spirit and instead start to focus on our institutional and intellectual structures we are pulled back by the dead weight of Dogma and fear'. But it need not be like that. There are endless riches in our God and there are innumerable people seeking for meaning and identity in life. Most of the time they find a Church which does not listen and turns in on itself.

Later in her poem Evelyn Underhill writes this:

He drives them east, he drives them west, between the dark
    and light;
He pastures them in city pens, he leads them home at night.
The towery trams, the threaded trains, like shuttles
    to and fro
To weave the web of working days in ceaseless travel go.
How harsh the woof, how long the weft!
Who shall the fabric see?
The one who walked with starry feet the western road by me!

It is as we look back we see that God is ever moving through the warp and weft of life that we see his coming in the things of daily life. It is our task as Christians not to point to ourselves but to seek the coming Christ in the complexity of ordinary life. Thus I have seen that my four children, who are not churchgoers but are all musicians and artists, that they are doing what they are doing for the same reasons that I got ordained. It is to seek value, justice and peace in human life and community and to see that God moves through all of this. So we see the God in that movement, at the heart of life and only he can see the whole picture.

As Evelyn Underhill ends:

Behold! he lent me as we went the vision of the seer;
Behold! I saw the life of men, the life of God shine clear.
I saw the hidden Spirit's thrust; I saw the race fulfil
The spiral of its steep ascent, predestined by the Will.
Yet not unled, but shepherded by one they may not see -
The one who walked with starry feet the western road by me!

Behold the Bridegroom cometh - go ye out to meet him.

A Thousand Years in Thy Sight is but as Yesterday

Christ Church Matins

Sunday 12th October 1997

Psalm 90, v. 2:
A thousand years in thy sight is but as yesterday, seeing that it is past as a watch in the night.

Those who know that they are dying rarely describe it, but in Philip Toynbee's journal *End of a Journey* we have exactly that. He knows he is dying of cancer. He describes life in the hospital and coming home to a refurbished bedroom for the last time. The very last entry in the journal reads:

> And I am again being pushed and pulled into this world without words, neither dreaming nor awake, neither moving towards God nor away from him.

Perhaps this is the nearest we shall get to understanding what it is like to die until it happens to us. A few paragraphs earlier he wrote:

> Vision of sweet sinking away, yet in full consciousness of life, death now seems much more remote. Must find some way of dying
> a) Not too fast
> b) As alert as possible
> c) As free of indigestion as possible
> d) As free of pain as possible

And that of course sums up much of the philosophy behind the hospice movement.

I have been driven to these reflections by thinking about that verse in our second lesson 2 Peter 3: v. 8 *'In the Lord's sight one day is like a thousand years and a thousand years like one day.'* The writer is here clearly reflecting on verse two from Psalm 90: *A thousand years in thy sight is but as yesterday, seeing that it is past as a watch in the night.*

Psalm 90 is a deeply reflective Psalm, which considers the transient nature of our being in comparison with God's eternal being. The Psalm reads like the thoughts of an old man looking back on his life

116

and seeing it as nothing compared to the timelessness of God. It moves to the affirmation that all life is finally rooted in God. The Psalm was attributed by some to Moses, reflecting at the end of his life. So it begins be seeing God is our refuge from one generation to another and sees that life can just pass way and ends by asking God to support and enrich the work of our life. It is not for nothing that this is one of the recommended psalms for a funeral. In other words, all our life, which seems so like a journey or a story with a beginning, a middle and an end is in fact all lived with the nowness of God.

We live with the mystery of time, a subject which has baffled scientists, philosophers and writers alike. We have only to think of J.B. Priestley's Time Plays to remind ourselves what a complex issue it is. People in biblical times did not see time in the same way as we do. As one writer has put it, from the Hebrew 'The past is what lies ahead and is therefore known; the future is unknown and is behind.'[81] Days went from sunrise to sunset. The Sabbath begins on Friday evening and ends at Saturday sunset. The word 'day' is often used as meaning a crucial moment. The night seems to have been divided into three 'watches', as we see in Psalm 90. But above all there is this deep contrast between our passing life and the eternity of God.

Some have seen in this verse the expectation of the end of all things. The thousand years is the millennium of God's reign. The weakness of this view was that nobody knew what the starting date was. So St. Augustine argued that the thousand years matched the time of the existence of the Church on earth. There are those now who expect something dramatic at the end of this millennium and this means we need to take due caution in how we think of this matter. Such thinking becomes an escape from the challenge of relating to God in the now.

Some people see eternity as something which goes on forever in a sort of an endless line, but the Biblical image as given in both our texts looks much more like a permanent now. In other words, God is, God always was 'is' and God always will be 'is'. Our task is to seek God in the present, to serve God in the present, to live in God's present and to die in his present. We see this in Toynbee's Journal: just after the piece about the means of dying, he writes:

> God must fill the whole mind again. Not in the sense of being actively thought about all the time - or even more than very rare and appropriate occasions. But I have learned better than ever in these last few weeks

81. Coogan, in Metzger, B.M. and Coogan. M.D. (eds) (1993) *The Oxford Companion to the Bible*, p. 744

how God can be truly in the mind, suffusing it and colouring all one's thoughts, hopes and actions - or grimly bleakly absent.

This matches the comment of Jaroslav Pelikan that 'The Gospel does not show a way round the fear of death but a way through the fear of death to life in God.'[82]

We see in Jesus' proclamation of the kingdom something which is upon us and a call to live as if God is ruling now. The challenge lies in the now.

From one point of view, we are all dying, there may be no future. Now is really all there is, and our way of life, our spirituality, our attitudes need to reflect this. We see it in the teaching of Jesus that we should not be anxious for the morrow but to trust in God's grace and mercy. It is as we reflect on our own mortality and God's eternal now, that we realise our own impotence and God's redeeming presence.

Such thinking led the 17th century Jesuit Jean Pierre de Caussaude to write in his letters to nuns of *The Sacrament of the Present Moment*. It is in the present moment that we encounter God. It is in the present moment that we respond to God. It is in the present moment that we either seek his will or reject it.

A thousand years in thy sight are but as yesterday, seeing that it is past as a watch in the night.

So perhaps we do need to have a greater sense of urgency, a greater sense of now and a less casual approach to the assumption that life can just go on and on. It should not be that it is only as we reach the moment of death we seek to let God fill the whole mind and that we need to be pulled either to or away from Him but to seek to rest in his presence. That is the essence of proper spirituality. For we die as we live, and the patterns of our living are matched in our dying.

---

82. Pelikan, J. (1961) *The Shape of Death: life, death and immortality in the early fathers*, New York: Abingdon Press

Thanksgiving Prayer for Bob Jeffery

O God, the Father of lights
and giver of every perfect gift
we hold in your presence the life of Bob Jeffery.

We remember his love for his family,
his care for his children, grandchildren and parents
and the creative, open-spirited home
that he and his wife Ruth made together.

We recall his humour and hospitality;
his love of cooking
his generosity with time and conversation
and we thank you for his friendship and counsel.

We thank you for Bob's ministry:
his work in the parishes of Grangetown, Barnes,
                    Headington and Tong,
his commitment to an outward-facing Church,
offering hope and refuge
for the downtrodden and oppressed
and we thank you for his teaching,
informed by a deeply practical spirituality.

We celebrate his stewardship of great buildings
and his love of history;
his work as Archdeacon of Salop, Dean of Worcester
and as Sub-Dean of Christ Church
his vision of restoring and repairing the fabric of great
churches
in order that they might be places for everyone.

Lord, your Gospel is one of reconciliation and unity.
We thank you for Bob's work towards the unity of your
Church;
And his understanding that
in both questioning and listening to each other
We may come to know your Kingdom more deeply.

We give thanks
that through these gifts
Bob came to know the abundant life
which is the promise of your Son,
asking that we too may learn
to trust more deeply
in that abiding promise;

for the sake of Him
who is the great shepherd of our souls,
Jesus Christ our Lord. Amen.

Bob Jeffery: Selected Publications

1965: with D.M. Paton, *Christian Unity and the Anglican Communion*, London: Church Information Office

1965: with T.S. Garret *Unity in Nigeria*, London: Edinburgh House Press

1968: *Lambeth Conference, 1968. Preparatory Information* (editor), London: SPCK

1968: *Areas of Ecumenical Experiment: a survey and report to the British Council of Churches*, London: British Council of Churches

1971: *Ecumenical Experiments: a handbook*, London: British Council of Churches

1980: (contrib.) Smith, M.L. (ed.) *Benson of Cowley*, Oxford: Oxford University Press

1987: (ed.) *By What Authority? The Open Synod Group report on authority in the Church of England*, London: Mowbray

1994: *Anima Christi: reflections on praying with Christ*, London: Darton, Longman and Todd

1995: (contrib.) *Coventry's First Cathedral: the Cathedral and Priory of St Mary: Anniversary symposium: papers*, Stamford: Paul Watkins

2002: (contrib.) Foust, T. F. (ed.) *A Scandalous Prophet: the way of mission after Newbigin*, Grand Rapids, Mich.: Eerdmans

2004: (contrib.) Chapman, M.D. (ed.) *Ambassadors of Christ: Commemorating 150 Years of Theological Education in Cuddesdon 1854 – 2004*, London: Routledge

2006: *Imitating Christ: Wesley's Christian Pattern and Spirituality for Today*, Tiverton: Methodist Sacramental Fellowship

2007: *Discovering Tong: its history, myths, and curiosities*, Tong: Tong P.C.C.

2007: (contrib.) Morgan, R. (ed.) *In Search of Humanity and Deity: a celebration of John Macquarrie's Theology*, London: SCM Press

2013: (translator) *The Imitation of Christ*, by Thomas A. Kempis, London: Penguin Classics

Bibliography: works cited

Adler, E. & Seiffert, L. (eds.) *'Pro-Existence': Christian Voices in East Germany 1954 – 1963*, London: SCM Press

ARCIC (1998) *The Gift of Authority*, http://www.vatican.va/roman_curia/pontifical_councils/chrstuni/documents/rc_pc_chrstuni_doc_12051999_gift-of-autority_en.html (accessed 29.05.17)

Barratt, P. (1993) *Barchester: English Cathedral Life in the Nineteenth Century*, London: SPCK

Baldwin, J. (1968): 'White Racism or World Community?' Address to the 1968 Uppsala Assembly of the World Council of Churches. Reported in *The Ecumenical Review* Vol. 22 No. 4, October 1968 p.375

Bethge, E. (2000) *Dietrich Bonhoeffer: Theologian, Christian, Man for His Times: A Biography*. Rev. ed. Minneapolis, Fortress Press

Bethge, E. (ed.), (1971, 3rd revised edition) *Dietrich Bonhoeffer: Letters and Papers from Prison, The Enlarged Edition*, London: SCM Press

Bonhoeffer, D., Doberstein, J.W (translator) (1954) *Life Together*, London: SCM Press

Bonhoeffer, D. (1995, 1st Touchstone ed.) *The Cost of Discipleship*, New York: Pocket Books

Borrie, G. *'Social Justice: the way ahead'* RSA Journal No 5457, March 1995

Bosch, D. (1991) *Transforming Mission: Paradigm Shifts in Theology of Mission*, Maryknoll, N.Y.: Orbis Books

Bosch, D. (1992) 'The Vulnerability of Mission.' *The Baptist Quarterly* NS 34 (1992) , no. 8: 351-63.

Bosch, D. (2006) *Witness to the World: the Christian Mission in Theological Perspective*, Eugene, OR: Wipf and Stock Publishers

Brecht, B., Willett, J. and Manheim, R. (eds.) (1979) *Poems 1913 -1956*, London: Methuen Drama

Brown, C. G. (2009, 2nd ed.) *The Death of Christian Britain: Understanding Secularization, 1800 – 2000* (Christianity and Society in the Modern World), London: Routledge

Buhlmann, W. (1976) *The Coming of the Third Church: an analysis of the present and future of the church*, Slough: St Paul Publications

Buhlmann, W., Smith, M. (translator) (1977) *Forward, Church!* Slough: St Paul Publications

Butterfield, H. (1957) *Christianity and History*, London: Fontana Books

Caussade, J.P., Muggeridge, K (translator) (1989 ed.) *The Sacrament of the Present Moment*, London: Harper Collins

Cullinan, T. (1974) *The Roots of Social Injustice.* London: Catholic Housing Aid Society

Davie, G. (1994): *Religion in Britain since 1945: Believing without Belonging* (Making Contemporary Britain), Oxford: Blackwell

Davie, G. (2015) *Religion in Britain: A Persistent Paradox*, Oxford: Wiley Blackwell

Davies. J.G. (1968) *The Secular Use of Church Buildings*, London: SCM Press

Derrett, J. D. M. (1973) *Jesus's Audience: The Social and Psychological Environment in Which He Worked: Prolegomena to a Restatement of the Teaching of Jesus, Lectures at Newquay 1971.* London: Darton, Longman and Todd

Doctrine Commission (1976): *Christian believing: the nature of the Christian faith and its expression in Holy Scripture and creeds*, London: SPCK

Doe, M. (2000) *Seeking the Truth in Love: the church and homosexuality*, London: Darton, Longman and Todd

Engel, U. (2007) *Worcester Cathedral: an architectural history*, Chichester: Phillimore

Gittins, A.J. (1999) *Reading the Clouds: Mission Spirituality for New Times*, Slough: St Paul Publications

Gray, J. 'The Sad Side of Cyberspace', *The Guardian*, 10.04.1995

Green, C.J. and DeJonge, M (eds.) (2013) *The Bonhoeffer Reader*, Minneapolis: Fortress

Gollwitzer, H., Cairns D. (translator) (1970) *The Christian Faith and the Marxist Criticism of Religion*, Edinburgh: St Andrew's Press

Harding, G. (1973) 'Death and Dying' *New Fire* No. 15, Summer 1973, p.289

Hopkins, G.M. (1985 ed.) 'That Nature is a Heraclitean Fire and of the comfort of the Resurrection', in *Poems and Prose*, Harmondsworth: Penguin Classics

Howe Commission (1994) Heritage and Renewal: *The Report of the Archbishops' Commission on Cathedrals*, London: Church of England

Jacob, B. (1997) *The Making of the Anglican Church Worldwide*, London: SPCK

Jenkins, D. (1990) *Still Living with Questions*, London: SCM Press

Kelly, G. B. and Nelson, F.B. (eds.) (1990) *A Testament to Freedom: The Essential Writings of Dietrich Bonhoeffer*, San Francisco: Harper

A Kempis, T. (2013 ed.), Jeffery, R.M.C (translator), *The Imitation of Christ*, London: Penguin Classics

Kirk, J. (1999) *What is Mission?* London: Darton, Longman and Todd

Küng, H. (2001, new ed.) *The Church*, London: Bloomsbury Publishing

Lash, N. (1988) *Easter in Ordinary: Reflections on Human Experience and the Knowledge of God*, Charlottesville: University Press of Virginia

Lehmberg, S.E. (1997) *Cathedrals Under Siege*, Exeter: Exeter University Press

McMaken, T. (2013) 'The Blame Lies with the Christians: Helmut Gollwitzer's engagement with Marxist Criticism of Religion', in *The Other Journal: an intersection of theology and culture*, April 2013.
https://theotherjournal.com/2013/04/22/the-blame-lies-with-the-christians-helmut-gollwitzers-engagement-with-marxist-criticism-of- religion/ (accessed 29.05.2017)

Moltmann, J., Meeks, M.D. (translator) (1978) *The Open Church: invitation to a messianic lifestyle*, London: SCM Press

Morton, T.R. (1957) *The Iona Community Story*, London: Lutterworth Press

Needham, J. (ed.) (1925) *Science, Religion and Reality*. London: Sheldon Press

Neill, S. (1964) *A History of Christian Missions*, (The Pelican History of the Church, Vol. 6), London: Pelican

Payne, J.D. (2003) 'The Legacy of Roland Allen', *Churchman* Vol. 117. No 4, pp. 315 – 328) http://archive.churchsociety.org/churchman/documents/Cman_117_4_Payne.pdf (accessed 29.05.17)

Pannikkar, R. (1964) *The Unknown Christ of Hinduism*, London: Darton, Longman and Todd.

Pelikan, J. (1961) *The Shape of Death: life, death and immortality in the early fathers*, New York: Abingdon Press

Poon, M. (2011) 'On Volatile Grounds: a history of church partnerships in Asia', in Poon, M.N-C. (ed.) *Church Partnerships in Asia: a Singapore conversation*, Singapore: Genesis Bools

Quick, O.C. (1927) *The Christian Sacraments*, London: Nisbet

Quick, O.C. (1938) *Doctrines of the Creed: Their Basis in Scripture and Their Meaning To-day*. London: Nisbet

Robinson, J.A.T (1963*) Honest to God*, London, SCM Press

Ruysbroeck, J.V., Underhill, E (ed.) (1916) *The Adornment of the Spiritual Marriage*, available at http://sacred-texts.com/chr/asm/index.htm (accessed 29.05.17)

Selby, P. (1991) *Belonging: challenge to a tribal church*, London: SPCK

Shannahan, C. (2016) *Voices from the Borderland: reimagining cross- cultural urban theology*, London: Routledge

Skelton, K. (1985) *Bishop in Smith's Rhodesia: Notes from a Turbulent Octave 1962 – 1970*, Gweru, Zimbabwe: Mambo Press

Society of St John the Evangelist (S.S.J.E) (1977) *The Rule for the Society of St. John the Evangelist, Oxford:* Cowley Publications 1997

126

Southcott, E.W. (1967, new impression) *The Parish Comes Alive,* London: Mowbray

Studdert Kennedy, G.A. (1927) *The Unutterable Beauty: the collected poetry of G.A. Studdert Kennedy,* London: Hodder and Stoughton

Sundkler, B. G.M. (1960) *The Christian Ministry in Africa,* London: SCM Press

Tacey, D (2000) *Re-enchantment: the new Australian spirituality,* Sydney: Harper Collins

Tacey D. (2004) *The Spirituality Revolution; the emergence of contemporary spirituality,* London: Routledge

Taylor, J.V. (1967) 'Training the Ordinand for Mission' in *International Review of Missions,* Vol. LVI, No. 22

Thomas, D. (1952) *Collected Poems 1934 – 1952,* London: J.M. Dent

Tillich, P. (2000, 2nd revised ed.) *The Courage to Be,* Yale: Yale University Press

Toynbee, P. (1988, 1st Bloomsbury ed.) *End of a Journey: an autobiographical journal 1979 – 81,* London: Bloomsbury

Underhill, E. (1917) 'Uxbridge Road', in Nicholson, F.H.S. and Lee, A.H.E. (eds.) (1932 ed.) *The Oxford Book of English Mystical Verse,* Oxford, Oxford University Press, p. 524

Van Engen, J. (translator) (1988) *Devotio Moderna: Basic Writings,* (Classics of Western Spirituality), New Jersey: Paulist Press

Van den Heuval, A.E. (1966): 'The functions of a cathedral in the community today 'in Papers read at a Conference of Deans and Provosts in Britain, held at Coventry Cathedral 22 – 25 April 1966, under the chairmanship of the Rev. Roger Lloyd.: Coventry Cathedral/Church of England

Vatican II (1964): *Lumen Gentium,* http://www.vatican.va/archive/hist_ councils/ii_ vatican_council/documents/vat-ii_const_19641121_lumen- gentium_en.html (accessed 29.05.17)

Vidal, G. (1987) *Armageddon? Essays 1983 – 1987,* London: Deutsch

Vincent, J. (1969) *Secular Christ: a contemporary interpretation of Jesus*, Nashville and New York: Abington Press

Vincent, J, and Rieger, J. (2004), *Methodist and Radical: rejuvenating a tradition*, Nashville, TN.: Abingdon Press

Vincent, J. (2004, revised edition) *Radical Jesus: the Way of Jesus, Then and Now*, Sheffield: Ashram Press

Weight, Richard, 'Return to Albion: Intellectuals in Wartime Britain', *History Today*, Vol. 44 (12) December 1994

Wilkinson, A. (1978) The Church of England and the First World War, London: SPCK

Williams, R. (1994) *Open to Judgement: selected sermons and writings*, London: Darton, Longman and Todd

Wilson, G. (1973) 'Why are Christians prejudiced?', *New Society*, 14th June 1973, p. 618

Wright, F. (1980) *The pastoral nature of the ministry*, London: SCM Press

A grove of trees has been planted in Scotland, in memory of Bob and Ruth Jeffery. Trees for Life is a charity that works to restore Scotland's ancient Caledonian Forest.

Anyone wishing to contribute a tree to the grove can donate here:

http://treesforlife.org.uk/plant-trees/grove/7574/